TO THE ENDS

OF THE EARTH

FOR MEREDITH, BEN, AND NICK

CONTENTS

FOREWORD

Alex Lowe

Author's note: This profile first appeared in Warren Miller's *SnoWorld* magazine just days after Alex was tragically killed in a Himalayan avalanche on October 5, 1999.

Alex Lowe in the cockpit of the C-130 just before landing on an ice runway in Queen Maud Land.

OPPOSITE: Alex Lowe solo climbs without a rope on a mountain in the Ellsworth Mountains he called Pyramid Peak.

THE BOARDED-UP WINDOWS RATTLE IN THE FRIGID DARKNESS and bits of siding, ripped loose by the wind, pound incessantly against the walls outside. The blizzard rages into its third night, the temperature registering -12°F (-11°C). I dread leaving the warmth of the dilapidated old fisherman's shack where we've holed up on Baffin Island's Remote Peninsula. But the venerable kerosene heater has run out of fuel again and it's my turn to plunge into the maelstrom and tap the fuel drum.

Reluctantly, I pull on mukluks, parka, goggles, and mitts. None of my companions stir except Gordon Wiltsie, who sits up in his sleeping bag and asks what I'm up to. Gordon is positively neurotic about photo opportunities, especially those evincing grim reality. So, dressing hastily, he follows me out.

"God," I think, "this guy is nuts."

I'd never leave my toasty bag to chase a photo into this godforsaken night. Outside, as I siphon kerosene, Gordon fires off a roll of film, his camera flash igniting the millions of snowflakes hurtling horizontally eastward. Each luminous explosion momentarily etched onto my retinas in the arctic night reminds me that once again I'm engaged in another wonderfully insane adventure with one of my favorite, wonderfully insane companions.

I first met Gordon in 1996. Imperiously paternalistic Montanans typically view transplants from the Golden State with disdain. But the Wiltsie family's arrival from their native Bishop, California, in 1992 was accepted as a serendipitous boon to the Bozeman community. I'd heard that Gordon was in town and knew of his well-founded reputation as the most adventurous adventure photographer in the business, but our paths had yet to cross.

I'd been invited to sail to Antarctica and climb along the peninsula that winter. Knowing that Gordon had been there, I phoned to solicit information on potential climbing objectives. We arranged a meeting over beers at a downtown bar and, although I didn't know what he looked like, Gordon was easy to spot. He walked in carrying a folder stuffed with photos, his ebullient gait and weather-beaten face clearly identifying him as a denizen of the earth's wooly places. As often happens with people I've met who have become compatriots in exploration, I immediately recognized a kindred spirit—someone possessing a shared lust to experience as much adventure as possible in the one precious pass we get at life.

Animated and enthusiastic, he divulged endless unexplored climbing objectives that evening and concluded by showing me photos of some of the most spectacular granite spires I've ever seen—the mountains of Antarctica's Queen Maud Land. We parted with a tacit agreement to climb together in this remarkable place. A year later I willingly embarked on the first of many shared odysseys. Often, I've reflected on that evening as one of the most fortuitous of my climbing career.

Gordon's a pretty amusing character, to say the least. Perhaps as a result of sixteen expeditions to the Arctic and Antarctic, the man is impervious to cold. In Queen Maud Land, we foolishly elected to spend the night in an open bivouac on a forlorn ridge. While the rest of us shivered the sleepless night away, Gordon sawed logs, curled on his side in the fetal position. Throughout the night we'd check his breathing to insure he hadn't succumbed to hypothermia. Occasionally he'd wake, remove his ever-present camera from the warmth of his parka, and fire pictures of the miserable lot of us huddled together for warmth. Then, to our envy and amazement, he'd settle back into comatose slumber.

Gordon definitely possesses a magnetic attraction for rocks—falling rocks. He narrowly escapes bombardment on every trip. Standing next to him at the base of a cliff is as comforting as standing beside a repeat lightning-strike victim as the cumulus clouds build on a hot August afternoon.

But photographic genius is Gordon's most extraordinary eccentricity. Through his camera lens, he captures far more than stunning mountain scenery and vivid climbing action. He conveys a complete story through his artistic imagery: struggle, elation, camaraderie and a gritty, honest portrayal of climbing accessible only to one who lives it himself. His unequaled ability to share an experience he knows intimately establishes Gordon as the quintessential adventure photographer.

Gordon's sons, Ben and Nick—already climbing circles around their dad—share what many kids might consider the ultimate father. Self-confident, extolling the dogged pursuit of dreams and possessing the creative energy to turn passion into vocation, Gordon provides a paternal mentor I would have worshiped as a budding young climber.

He fell in love with and mastered two demanding pursuits at an early age—exploration and photography. Talent, determination, and the devotion of Meredith, his wife and business partner, have sublimated these obsessions into a lifestyle that perpetuates both.

OPPOSITE: Gordon Wiltsie.

PHOTO BY ALEX LOWE

PREFACE

ANYONE FLIPPING THROUGH THE PHOTOGRAPHS I have shot for magazines over the past thirty years might think that I've lived a life that borders on the sublime. There are startling images of world-class mountaineers scaling spectacular Antarctic cliffs; weather-beaten nomads leading yaks, sheep, or camels through deep snow over remote Asian passes; magic light dancing across vistas that anyone would be grateful to have seen.

I have been blessed to tag along with remarkable people who continue to explore a planet of astonishing beauty and power. Except for goofing off with my family, there is nothing I love more than journeying to spectacular wilderness landscapes and capturing my companions' exploits on film for others to see. This passion has brought great meaning to what otherwise might have been a rudderless life. I have always found contact with a higher power in the mountains. Like many another preacher moved by the spirit, I have long been obsessed with proselytizing my alpine epiphanies.

As a youngster I seldom went to church. But even from an early age I could see that the magnificent natural wonders of places such as the Sierra Nevada were as close to perfection as anything else I might ever see. If asked to define my higher power, I'd still say that it is something like the light that shines onto a lenticular cloud at sunset, exploding the sky into a fleeting burst of glory. It is the life force creeping up the capillaries of a 4,800-year-old bristlecone pine, twisting and shaping it into something as beautiful as anything sculpted by humans. Ever since I started recognizing such things, I have tried to capture them on celluloid; to show what I thought was "the way" to others.

If one believes in such concepts as karma or dharma, perhaps I was destined to follow the path that I did. I grew up in the shadow of 14,000-foot (4,270-meter) peaks, and my parents loved nothing better than wilderness expeditions. I discovered rock climbing and met two pillars of mountain journalism, Doug Robinson and Galen Rowell, within a year of becoming a

Sam Lightner descends a slot canyon below huge Shiptons Arch in Tushuk Tash Mountains, Xinjiang, China.

Golomianiy Weather Station beside the Arctic Ocean on Russia's Severnaya Zemlya archipelago.

photographer for my high school yearbook. Mere chance? I don't think so. Like many of my peers starting college in 1970, traditional careers seemed remarkably unsatisfying and this impetus propelled me to seek a life in the mountains.

The quest became obsessive for me, involving struggles and setbacks that are far beyond the scope of this book. Throughout this process, however, one transition was especially notable. In the beginning, I defined myself as an "outdoor" or an "adventure" photographer. Today I use the term "expedition photographer." Although the differences are subtle, they're important—a measure of my growth both as an image maker and a person able to juggle the often contradictory worlds of finance, politics, and the extremes of nature.

Adventure photography can be just an afternoon jaunt. Expedition photography, on the other hand, is a far more complicated exploratory endeavor that may be very expensive, involve years of planning, and invoke risks far beyond what most people would consider acceptable. I, myself, have far outlived my own ration of nine lives.

The boundary between an adventure and an expedition is primarily an order of magnitude—akin to the difference between a basic education and a doctorate. In order to safely join expeditions, one needs significant experience with related adventures. In my own case, for example, it would have been impossible to undertake any of my polar expeditions without years spent guiding rock climbing and ski mountaineering groups close to home in the Sierra Nevada. Similarly, my success covering an epic migration in Mongolia stemmed from experiences traveling alone in Asia, first as an exchange student living with a Nepalese family, then as a newlywed, on honeymoon with my wife, Meredith, when we worked on rehabilitation projects for starving people in Bangladesh. It was these, along with other eclectic adventures—including trekking around Annapurna without a map, just weeks after this now-classic route opened to foreigners—that gave me the confidence to join my first-ever "real" expedition, the one that is the first chapter of this book.

Now, after photographing some of earth's wildest and least-known places—some never before visited by humans—part of me is proud. I know that my work has been useful in helping to protect places I love. My pictures of Antarctica, for example, may have helped to convince some members of the U.S. Senate to ratify a stricter, more environmentally sensitive treaty governing the continent; a magazine filled with my words and images was sent to every Senator shortly before the vote. I also have played a minor role in the explosive growth of rock climbing, backcountry skiing, and adventure travel—developments that I have long considered vital to the appreciation and subsequent preservation of wild places and disappearing cultures of the world.

I know that a few of my pictures and stories have inspired people. I get letters, e-mail, and phone calls telling me so. Almost every week I hear from college students and young adventurers who seek to build a career like mine (or, perhaps, their vision of mine). They beg me for a curriculum, an off-road map that will lead them to a life of adventure at the edges of the earth. Sadly, such a map does not exist. Insofar as each rising photojournalist has to find his or her own way to an elusive measure of "success," the path to becoming a brain surgeon or professional football player is

The Potala Palace in Lhasa, Tibet, was formerly home to the Dalai Lama and remains a shrine today. Under Chinese occupation, much has changed since I took this picture in 1986. The prayer flags are gone and high-rise buildings now dominate the city.

Tibetan Buddhist monks take a break from their studies at Drepung Monastery, near Lhasa.

arguably more direct than that to a *National Geographic* photographer!

Expedition photography is especially difficult, in that it requires not just experience with mountaineering, skiing, dog sledding, jungle travel, or desert survival, but also mastery of using a camera in the very kinds of circumstances when the last thing you want to do is to take photographs. Given the ever-increasing visual sophistication of photographic viewers, the old adage of "f/11 and be there" doesn't cut it anymore. Even in the worst conditions you need flashes, sophisticated camera techniques, and a rock-solid understanding of the way cameras "think" and see.

Given the numbers of people who want to become adventure or expedition photographers, one needs passion and perseverance, as well. Nowadays one of the first questions I ask my photography students is "How badly do you want this?" Then I follow up with "Are you willing to risk everything, including your family, your freedom, and your life?"

Finally, and perhaps most importantly, an expedition photographer has to build an astonishing network of friends and colleagues. This is a lifelong process, with one introduction or event leading inexorably to the next, in an ever-more-complicated network of relationships and actions that I choose to call karma. Whether or not this has consequences in an afterlife, it certainly affects how things go in this one. I've found that if I respect people, treat them as I would like to be treated myself, and behave honestly to both the world

Pilgrims line up to view temples at the Potala Palace in 1986. Tourists are no longer allowed to visit the palace when large numbers of Tibetans are present.

and myself, dreams have a chance to come true. And this brings me to a different kind of truth, one of my underlying reasons for writing this book.

As honest as I have always tried to be, my pictures do not always tell the whole story. Sometimes they are illusions of a world that, as time passes and my memories fade, fool even me. Every photograph I take, for example, involves some form of conscious manipulation. I choose a particular lens or a certain film, and frame each shot, making decisions about what to put in and what to leave out. I can suck backgrounds in close and sharp, or make them disappear in a distant blur. I can add artificial light, tilt the camera, and do many other things to coax you into feeling how I want you to feel about my subjects. I never actually try to "lie"—in fact, I always try to do quite the opposite—but like any visual artist, I am constantly tempted to show only what I want you to see.

Above and beyond lenses, f-stops, and composition, I think that another tough part of my job is choosing exactly when to trip my shutter. Many of the photographs I am proudest of depict fleeting facial expressions, apogees of physical exertion, or flashes of momentary light that lasted a mere fraction of a second, then disappeared forever. Whether I carefully calculate each exposure or rapidly fire away with a motor drive, there is often but a single frame that captures the essence of that moment. I never show the rest to anyone. Usually I throw them away.

1

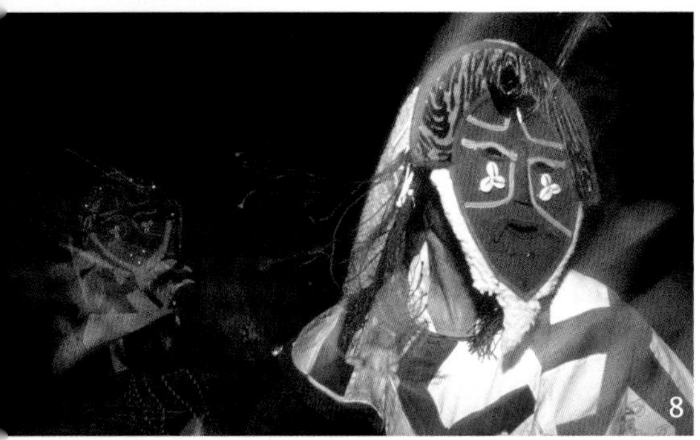
8

7

6

5

2

3

4

9

13

10

12

11

One of my favorite images, for example, depicts a loving Tibetan couple exchanging an intimate glance. In the photograph they appear to be totally alone. In truth they were in a vast crowd that parted for mere seconds, allowing me to isolate them with a telephoto lens. You don't see the beggar tugging at my sleeve, or feel my fear of being arrested by the Chinese police, much less my loneliness, and my worries that staying away from home so long might be harmful to my family.

Tibetan villagers circle the Jokhang Temple during a pilgrimage to Lhasa.

Ultimately, my photo file is a ruthlessly edited version of what I have seen and experienced over the years. I have long since lost accurate count, but at least two thousand of my pictures have been published, some many times over. If I had shot these at an average shutter speed of 1/60th of a second, the core of my life's work consists of barely thirty seconds' worth of exposed film—one second for every year of my career! Even if I add up every frame I have ever cranked through a camera, include all the trash, the total would be less than a million slides—less than five minutes of decisive creativity.

Of course, most people recognize that creating a good photograph involves a lot more time than the brief instants I spend opening the shutter. There are, too, many individual pictures that took more than thirty seconds each. But I'm pretty sure that the young people who write to me, earnestly imagining a career as an outdoor photographer, have little idea of just how much happens in the countless hours between those essential clicks.

I am writing this book for several reasons. At this point in my career, I want to display in one place some of my favorite images. I have chanced upon widely diverse opportunities, and if only for my own pleasure, I'd like to see the pictures presented side by side, demonstrating (I hope!) my evolving vision of the world and increasing technical ability to capture it.

I also want to step out of the shadows. On numerous occasions, my photography has helped other people to achieve enormous fame, while I shuffle unseen in their umbra. My personal expeditionary efforts often get overlooked or ignored in their subsequent storytelling. I accept that this is a price of my job, but part of the reason I can create the pictures I produce is that I am usually a full-fledged team member. I carry loads (in addition to my camera gear), set up tents, belay, cook, wash dishes, and otherwise do my share. The benefit is that my subjects take me so much for granted that they forget my camera and consider me just another comrade. I can sit there, in plain sight—just like the proverbial fly on the wall—

and fire away. Now I want to look back and tell a few famous adventure stories (and some that aren't famous at all) as I saw them unfold. To tell the story as honestly as possible, I've mixed in some of the previously unpublished photographs, and have woven together my recollections from journals, pictures, and letters recorded at the time. I want to avoid judgmental hindsight; I do not want to glare back like some older and wiser Grand Inquisitor and bark "Were you crazy?" I'd rather tell this with my passion of the moment—in love with cameras that could tell a story.

Alex Lowe leads the Triple Indirect route on Table Mountain above Cape Town, South Africa, while waiting for a flight to Queen Maud Land, Antarctica.

1

2

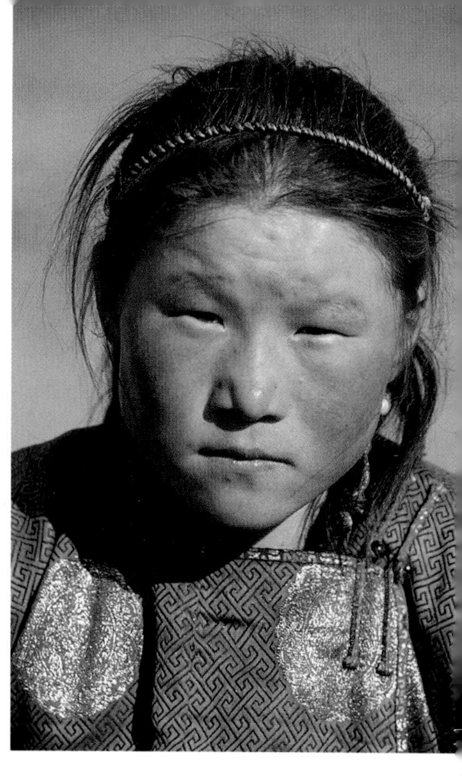

8

7

6

9

10

11

16

12

15

14

13

TO THE ENDS OF THE EARTH

GETTING STARTED

1952–1979

Sunset light on an ancient bristlecone pine in the White Mountains above Bishop.

OPPOSITE: A high altitude "Sierra Wave" over Owens Valley.

- ***Base Camp:*** My birthplace, Bishop, California; 37° N, 118° W; halfway between Los Angeles, California, and Reno, Nevada. Bishop sits in the remote Owens Valley—America's deepest—nestled between the towering eastern escarpment of the Sierra Nevada to the west and the White Mountains, which soar nearly as high, less than 20 miles (35 km) to the east
- ***Dates:*** August 4, 1952, until late August 1992, when Meredith, my children, and I moved to Bozeman, Montana
- ***Prominent characters***: My parents, David and Patricia Wiltsie; high school classmates Jay Jensen, Roger Schley, Bill Albright, and Bill Denton; various mountaineers, including Doug Robinson and Galen Rowell; Meredith, Ben, and Nick Wiltsie; numerous foreign friends

MY PASSION FOR WILD PLACES WAS SEALED by growing up beneath at least ten 14,000-foot (4,270 m) peaks. I was a few months old when my parents first took me to 11,000 feet (3,350 m), and in ensuing years we undertook many family expeditions to wilderness places, including long canoe trips to remote lakes in eastern Canada. By age thirteen, I thought that it was normal to slog all day under a heavy pack, boil up a meager dinner, then shiver all night in a drenched, cotton sleeping bag atop a punctured air mattress in a tent that leaked like a colander.

When I was a sophomore in high school I earned an Eagle Scout badge. I was also a well-behaved student and seemed destined for a promising future. Then, during my junior year, I became a photographer and writer for both the school newspaper and the yearbook. This made me popular (jocks love to have their pictures taken), and I began to reassess my future. Meanwhile, Bill Albright and Bill Denton, whom I had known as long as I could talk, had recently discovered climbing. They gave me a few lessons and the sport resonated with a rebellious spirit buried deep within me. As hard as I subsequently tried to be "normal," my life never would be the same again.

My high school friends, Jay Jensen and Roger Schley, who helped introduce me to mountaineering, warm themselves by campfire in the Sierra Nevada near Bishop. They are dressed entirely in wool, the best available fabric at the time.

AN AUSPICIOUS ENCOUNTER

Someday after school, October 1969 (age 17)

■ ***Location:*** The Chalk Bluff cliffs, 10 miles (17 km) northwest of Bishop

Amid Bishop's first candlelight rally against the Vietnam War (an explosive event for the rednecks in town), Bill, Bill, and I met our first-ever real hippie, an elfish, bearded guru named Doug Robinson. Each of us had read Doug's transcendental articles in prominent climbing publications such as *Summit,* and the Sierra Club's *Ascent* (two early members of the genre that now includes *Outside, Backpacker,* and *National Geographic Adventure*), and we couldn't believe such a famous writer was so approachable and eager to teach us.

He took us bouldering on huge, round rocks he called The Peabodies, and he taught us how to keep ourselves alive on longer routes, where he proselytized a new environmentally sensitive school of climbing he had defined in a recent essay as "clean." Then one afternoon he takes us to a short, off-width crack that splits two dihedral slabs on which someone long ago painted GET RIGHT WITH GOD and JESUS IS COMING SOON, REPENT. The graffiti is prominent from US 395, and the land is owned by one of my former Boy Scout leaders. Rumors whispered that he had chased away other climbers with a shotgun.

Doug scoots right up the crack. Then it's my turn. But what seems easy to him is impossible for me. I grapple and gasp, but however I wind my arms and feet into the fissure, no position promotes upward mobility. Meanwhile, I'm looking over my shoulder for "Mr. Scoutmaster, Sir." Instead, a speeding white Chevy station wagon squeals a U-turn off the highway. Out jumps a seemingly crazy man wielding a Nikon. Doug shouts a greeting from above and introduces us to Galen Rowell, a twenty-seven-year-old car mechanic and photographer from Berkeley who is even more famous than Doug. We youngsters have all read Galen's epic stories and seen his pictures, and we feel as if we're in the presence of gods.

Still, they seem perfectly human. We regroup beneath the crack and listen to them trade tales about this and that. I've recently dreamed of making a living in the mountains, and these two are succeeding. If they can do it, why can't I?

Cattle graze below the eastern escarpment of the Sierra Nevada, where Mounts Emerson, Humphreys, and Basin (left to right) rise nearly two vertical miles above the Owens Valley floor.

Doug Robinson climbs on one of the Peabody Boulders, near Bishop, California.

Doug Robinson climbs the Get Right with God crack.

Stormy sunrise on the east face of 14,494 foot (4,419 m) Mount Whitney, highest point in the contiguous forty-eight states.

Copper Bazaar, Adana, Turkey

TROUBLE IN TURKEY

Mid-February, 1973 (age 20)

■ ***Location:*** Göreme Valley, Turkey; 38° N, 34° E; 140 miles (235 km) southeast of Ankara

"I love you," says Ahmed, swinging beefy arms around me and kissing me with hashish-scented breath. "I want to show you the most secret caves of Anatolia." He's a swarthy man about half-again my age, surrounded by five goons who look like they want to pummel me, steal my passport, and drive away in my Volkswagen van. Even though I am only twenty and therefore generally feel invincible, the setting—which I imagine resembles those in which fellow vagabonds simply "disappear"—seems inauspicious.

Nevertheless, I've become addicted to adrenaline, and this is the biggest rush so far on my first solo foreign journey. As a person coming of age in the tumultuous early seventies, I believed that I had to reject traditional middle-class life and pursue a wilder ride. Instead of becoming a climbing bum, however, I took a year off from my chemistry major at Amherst College in Massachusetts to swab a grimy floor at a mine, hack out U.S. Forest Service trails, and earn enough money to buy a battered van and spend six months traveling in Europe. Now, after motoring through the Alps and down Yugoslavia's scenic Dalmatian Coast into Greece, I'm across the Bosporus in Asia and have never felt so alone.

Ahmed is obviously in rut and I have to escape. But he is sitting in my passenger seat and his entourage lounges on my homemade bed behind us, sneering and puffing cigarettes. I try to think fast. "I'd love to go with you," I lie, "but my girlfriend is flying into Istanbul tonight and I have to pick her up." I know that he knows that it's at least a ten-hour drive.

He looks crestfallen, but also ready to grab me. I try to sound as silken tongued as he is. "Both of us will come right back and take your tour. This is the most interesting place in Turkey!" I hope that lascivious wheels will turn in his reptilian brain, lusting not only after me, but also some nonexistent bombshell blonde. Then a policeman walks by, jostling his machine gun and eyeing us suspiciously.

"Alright," he sighs. "I will see you soon! Promise me." He turns and silently gestures for his friends to depart. "I do love you," he says, and opens his door. I jam the transmission into first and lurch forward, vowing never to return.

This Yugoslavian peasant chose her own pose after I "earned" the right to photograph her by carrying several loads of hay into her barn near Dubrovnik.

A NEPALESE PERSPECTIVE

Mid-May 1974 (age 21)

LOCATION: ***Arubari, Nepal; 27º N, 85º E; amid rice paddies 5 miles (8 km) northeast of Kathmandu***

"*Tapain le himal charye?*" asks Kalika Risal, a high-caste Hindu rice farmer whom I call *Ba* ("father"). He is appalled that I have willingly solo climbed a 20,000-foot (6,100 m) mountain in the fearsome "Abode of Snow" above his home. He is also shocked that I have proudly befriended untouchable Sherpa hicks.

My European travels have shown me that few people think like the people I knew back home. Now I am even farther away. After returning home from Turkey, I transferred to the University of California, Santa Cruz, where I quickly learned about a foreign study program that my only sibling, Anne, was joining in Nepal. I changed my major to creative writing and photojournalism and tagged along. Now, after living for almost four months with a family that doesn't speak English, I have finished my dinner of rice and lentils, and Ba's older wife, Yesodra, is using cow dung to purify the floor where my plate had been. I realize that there is such a gulf between our cultures that I can't explain my mountain behavior to anyone in the room.

After I solo climbed the south summit of Island Peak, I looked back to see Ang Rita Sherpa, who had carried my pack to base camp, following me at a distance and slipping wildly because he had no crampons. Here, after climbing his very first mountain, he enjoys a cigarette at about 20,000 feet (6,100 m).

Kalika Risal and his granddaughter, Sarwada.

While I was in Nepal, Doug Robinson sent some of my black-and-white photography to *Mountain Gazette,* a literary magazine. During my absence, the editor published several of those images, including one on the cover. Later, he also printed my first-ever feature article, "All in the Family," a story with pictures about my adventures with Ba.

Gordon Wiltsie leads a pitch on Lucifer's Ledge, Glacier Point, Yosemite National Park. PHOTO CREDIT: DOUG ROBINSON

MY FIRST BIG WALL

Mid-June 1974 (age 21)

■ ***Location:*** Northwest Face, Half Dome, Yosemite National Park; 38° N, 120° W

"Screw the camera and keep the rope tighter!" screams Jay Jensen, my high school buddy who is usually as solid as the concrete his father is teaching him to pour for a living. We're at least 1,500 feet (460 m) straight off the ground, and I have just finished leading one of the scariest pitches on this legendary climb. We are attempting to ascend the wall "clean," a feat that has only been accomplished once before, by a team that included Galen and Doug, and that was considered notable enough to earn Galen his first cover story for *National Geographic.*

Meanwhile, Jay is now halfway across horrifying Thank God Ledge, which divides two absolutely blank, near-vertical walls and is too narrow to walk. As he was halfway through hand-over-handing about fifty feet (15 m) due sideways, I foolishly asked him to lean out for a picture. Meanwhile, his own attention was divided between the vast maw below him and the big, square-cornered dihedral into which he would pendulum and splat should he fall. Earlier, when he cut loose our haul bag, it arced into an awe-inspiring swing and nearly exploded when it slammed into the same obstacle. Worse, two days earlier, we watched another climber get rescued after he catapulted into a similar dihedral two pitches below.

I feel Jay start moving so quickly that I can scarcely pull in the rope fast enough. He scrambles on to my ledge and we realize we're going to make it. His rush of adrenaline fades. "I should shove that camera right down your throat," he grins. "You got the shot, didn't you?" (I didn't.)

Jay Jensen leads a pitch above Thank God Ledge, Half Dome, Yosemite National Park.

Meredith Nelson crosses French Pass during her first wilderness ski tour.

THE DATE FROM HELL (ME)

Spring Break, 1975 (age 22)

■ ***Location:*** Paiute Pass, John Muir Wilderness; 37° N, 119° W; 15 miles (24 km) east of Bishop

"Meredith," I say, trying to hide my exasperation. "The point of skiing is *not* to fall down!" Fifty feet (15 m) above me—too far for me to climb up and help her—my new girlfriend lies cratered deep in fresh-fallen snow, buried beneath a fifty-pound (25 kg) pack. I know it's going to take her at least five minutes to dig out, shake loose any snow that's sneaked beneath her wool clothing, and start back down again.

Meredith has seldom skied before and I have foolishly invited her to join Jay Jensen, me, and several other backcountry-hardened friends on a remote winter tour, high in the Sierra Nevada. For four excruciating days we have been slogging up long hills—and sliding back down—on waxed, wooden skis that are attached to leather mountain boots with non-releasable cable bindings.

I've known Meredith Nelson only a few months now, but am already in love with her perceptive insights, bright blue eyes, and infectious giggle. I sense that we're made for each other and want to introduce her to the world I love, including my eccentric friends, a band of skiers and climbers who call themselves "The Armadillos." One of them, Roger Schley, lives in a tepee, and most have dropped out of school to pursue a life closer to the Earth. Still a student, I envy them and wish that I, too, could head into the mountains on a whim, leaving my cares behind. I'm certain that Meredith will feel the same.

Unfortunately, things are not going as planned. Snow has dogged us for most of the trip, and each night we've been stuffed into a leaky tent with the other guys, all of whom reek like wet sheep. Only well into the journey does it occur to me that she might find this less than romantic, and now things are going slowly downhill—in a very literal sense. Halfway down our long, unexpectedly steep descent to the road, she is crashing every turn and I wonder if we'll make it down before dark. Our companions are nowhere to be seen.

Finally, just as the stars begin to twinkle brightly, we reach our car. Our friends have been waiting for hours. Meredith takes off her boots and socks. Her heels look like they've been filed by a wood rasp. I'm almost certain that she'll never speak to me again, but if she does, I've found the love of my life.

HONEYMOON IN BANGLADESH

May 22, 1977 (age 24)

■ ***Location:*** Dhaka International Airport, Dhaka, Bangladesh; 24° N, 90° E

"Mr. Gordon, show me your passport!" barks a big, ugly man as I walk into departure customs with my young wife, Meredith. He flashes a badge that reads MR. HASSAN and sneers "Open your bags!" Fear overwhelms me. How can he already know my name?

Meredith and I had married just four months earlier, dreaming of traveling the world as a writer-photographer team. To help finance our "honeymoon," Meredith had discovered that we could earn free airfare to Asia by agreeing to volunteer for three months in a beggar's rehabilitation camp outside Dhaka.

After swearing that neither of us was a journalist and that we wouldn't work in the country, we landed in the struggling young nation shortly after its bloody war of independence, which had been followed by a typhoon and tsunami. Together, these catastrophes left hundreds of thousands of people dead, millions homeless, and much of the nation's intelligentsia executed—their wives raped and wealth carried away to Pakistan. Bangladesh was on its knees, ruled by a ruthless military junta.

For ten hours a day, six days a week, we toiled in tropical heat at Mirpur Destitute Camp, where several thousand people crammed their scant remaining possessions into a bombed-out soap factory. Never before had we witnessed families so desperate, and we slaved to make a difference. With only rudimentary, self-taught Bengali, Meredith gave lessons in hygiene, nutrition, and family planning to teenage girls who had already borne several children. Meanwhile, I helped some of the camp's few men and older boys clean up a fetid pond so they could start cooperatively raising fish. Every noon we handed out donated survival biscuits and Carnation Instant Slender, and each evening we each wrote page after page of journal notes that we thought were destined to become a book. Then, just as we felt like we were beginning to accomplish something, Bengali Immigration refused to renew our "tourist" visas.

"If you are really a tourist," Hassan demands, "why did you stay in Bangladesh so long?" He burrows into my duffle bag and pulls out my entire stack of journals—about a thousand pages of painstakingly written notes that document all manner of suffering, cruelty, and corruption. He also grabs my bag of exposed film: everything I haven't already sent home with a friend. "I'm going to keep these," he says. "We've been watching you, and I think that you're a journalist. Or are you a spy?"

Women from Mirpur Destitute Camp listen to a family planning lecture.

I protest, but Meredith stares me down. Finally, Hassan seems convinced that I am both sufficiently intimidated and too naive to be much of a threat to Bangladesh, especially without my film and notes. He says that unless I'd like to wait until he has processed and studied everything, we can leave without them. We run to catch our plane to Kathmandu, which has now been waiting for more than an hour. Meredith is near tears, but can't suppress a wan smile. She unzips her daypack, which Hassan never checked, and reveals her own writing, some fifteen hundred pages. She sighs grimly. "I'll bet he thinks that I can't even read!"

The cattle market near Mirpur, a suburb of Dhaka.

HIGHWAY TO HEAVEN

Eve of the full moon, August 1977 (age 25)

■ ***Location:*** Mahagunas Pass, Great Himalaya Range, Kashmir; 34° N, 75°E; a half-day's walk from Amarnath Cave, where Shiva imparted the secret of immortality to his consort, Parvati

"Since I choose not to fly and you cannot, I will walk with you," suggests Narayan Giri, grabbing his begging bowl and pulling on his trident, a symbol of Shiva, to stand. Even though we have been sitting at 15,100 feet (4,600 m) elevation, he is stark naked, covered only in ash. Long, tangled dreadlocks reach nearly to his waist and his hands are black with hashish that he has been rubbing off ganja leaves growing beside the trail. He's shared enough of it with me that I feel as if I have already taken flight. This is a pilgrimage, and cannabis is simply part of the ritual. Even a middle-aged banker from Delhi, dressed in slacks and a sports shirt, has joined us.

Since fleeing Bangladesh, Meredith and I have spent many weeks trekking in the Himalaya. Just after arriving in Kathmandu, for example, we set off with a single Tibetan porter to become two of the first Westerners to hike around Annapurna, a route that we were certain would one day become a classic. Despite leeches probing from every trailside bush and monsoon clouds that drenched us daily, we were entranced by the route's ever-changing landscapes and cultures.

ABOVE: A village near Muktinath, north of Annapurna.

RIGHT: Children celebrating Gai Jatra festival in Kathmandu.

Hindu pilgrims cross 15,100-foot (4,600 m) Mahagunas Pass, en route to Amarnath Cave.

A wealthy Hindu woman travels to Amarnath Cave in a sedan chair borne by Islamic Kashmiri porters.

Hindu pilgrims crush toward Amarnath Cave at dawn, immediately following the set of the full moon.

In less than a month we passed through dense rhododendron forests, traversed what may be the world's deepest gorge (the Kali Gandaki, between 26,545-foot [8,091 m] Annapurna and 26,795-foot [8,167 m] Dhaulagiri), crossed a 17,700-foot (5,400 m) pass, descended into another deep valley where our porter was certain we would be robbed, and finally re-emerged into vast, rolling hills carved by generations of farmers into thousands of iridescent green rice paddies. Every bend in the trail revealed new photographs, and for the first time in my life, I started shooting more color film than black-and-white.

more than thirty thousand people of every description have flocked from across the subcontinent to hike four days over two high passes in order to pray to Shiva. Side by side with us are sadhus like Narayan Giri, normal-looking middle-class families, old women hobbling with canes, cripples with elephantiasis, rich matrons riding in sedan chairs borne by half a dozen Muslim porters, trains of ponies carrying steamer trunks, and countless others in a cavalcade mirroring all the mystery of Hinduism.

Except for a few hippies pretending to be sadhus, we're the only Westerners. Still, we feel safe and few people object as I shoot hundreds of photographs for what I am certain will be a perfect feature for *Outside*, a new magazine that Doug Robinson has told me is about to be launched.* Meredith and I swear that this is exactly what we want to do for the rest of our lives.

* *Outside* did, in fact, later publish a story about the pilgrimage that Meredith and I wrote together, accompanied by my pictures. It was our first color feature in any national magazine.

If Annapurna was exotic, our present setting is surreal. As far as we can see on either side of the pass, a vast human procession is marching deeper into the mountains, plodding four abreast in a line that stretches for miles. We have happened upon one of the biggest *yatras* (mountain pilgrimages) in India:

A Hindu sadhu meditates at temple in Kathmandu.

Baruntse Peak. After climbing a 2,500-foot (750 m) headwall that is out of frame, our route goes up the left skyline of this picture.

CHAPTER ONE

INNOCENTS AT ALTITUDE

Learning Expedition Ropes, Baruntse Peak, Nepal, 1980

- ***Location:*** Baruntse Peak and environs, Khumbu region, Nepal; 27° N, 87° E; the valleys below Mounts Everest and Lhotse
- ***Team:*** Dr. Peter Hackett (leader), John Fischer, Jay Jensen, Gordon Wiltsie, and Lanny Johnson and Richard Collins, who taught at the Sherpa climbing seminars.
- ***Dates:*** August 10 to October 20, 1980
- ***Conditions:*** Everything from tropical heat, high humidity, and thunderstorms to Himalayan blizzards with temperatures far below 0°F (−20°C) and winds above 100 mph (165 kph)

DURING THE FALL OF 1974, an ambitious young doctor named Peter Hackett trekked into Nepal's Khumbu region, south of Mount Everest. En route he discovered that hikers were falling gravely ill, even perishing, from poorly understood symptoms of high-altitude sickness. Fascinated, Peter began work at a primitive new clinic founded by the Himalayan Rescue Association in Pheriche village, alongside the trail to Everest base camp. He quickly began treating stricken adventurers and also accumulating data that would lead to significant medical breakthroughs. In addition, he occasionally led treks for Mountain Travel, a pioneering adventure-travel company.

Several years later, during the monsoon and winter seasons when few people trek or climb, Peter also began work in the emergency room at Northern Inyo Hospital in Bishop, California, the very place where I was born. There he met many young climbers, including me, my high school friend Jay Jensen, and John Fischer, who owned a prominent local climbing school for which both Jay and I had worked. Like Peter, John and I already had led treks into the Khumbu for Mountain Travel, and the four of us dreamed of climbing a mountain there.

If any of us had cajoled the right people, we probably could have joined one of the huge, siege-style Himalayan expeditions that pillars of the American Alpine Club organized every year, but we wanted something different. We wanted to go just as friends, under casual circumstances where we didn't have to be bossed around by alpha climbers whose names we read in every alpine publication. We believed that mountaineering was more than simply reaching a summit; our trip should include the same spirit of fun and camaraderie we felt hiking up the trail and cracking jokes around the campfire back home.

A Tibetan Buddhist *mani* (prayer) stone. The inscription reads "Om mani padme hum," Hail to the Jewel in the Lotus, a mantra spoken throughout the Himalaya.

While debating which mountain to attempt (we were too inexperienced to challenge one of the legendary 8,000-meter peaks by ourselves), Peter mentioned 23,680-foot (7,220 m) Baruntse, which towers above Island Peak and had only been climbed once in the 1950s during a research expedition led by Sir Edmund Hillary. Peter had already sweet-talked a pilot into flying over its summit, and showed us pictures that suggested we might be able to ski down Baruntse's southern ridge. Far more difficult than climbing and skiing Baruntse, we thought, would be raising the money to attempt it.

None of us had any experience with fund-raising, and we spent two years wooing sponsors. To our surprise, it was easy to arrange clothing and equipment. Himalayan skiing was an unusual new twist, and I had published enough in outdoor magazines and catalogs that companies viewed us as a relatively cheap way to get exciting photographs of their products in action. To earn our airfare three of us promised to lead at least one post-expedition trek for Mountain Travel. To generate cash for food, porters, and myriad other expenses, we sold T-shirts, showed films, and asked some of our former guiding clients for support. Then Peter had an epiphany.

He realized that every year dozens of Sherpas were killed or injured while supporting expeditions. This resulted in part from their repeated trips through dangerous icefalls, but equally from a lack of training in technical mountaineering. Because of the Sherpas' amazing lung power and inherent physical agility, most expedition leaders simply assumed that they knew all about knots, belaying, rappelling, ice ax self-arrests, crevasse rescues, and other skills that even intermediate climbers take for granted. Peter, however, had learned that they did not. Though it seemed like selling refrigerators to Eskimos, he suggested that we seek donations to conduct a climbing school for Sherpas. We mailed a fund-raising letter to everyone we could imagine, and because Sherpa people are beloved by almost all who encounter them, checks poured in. By August 1980 we were funded, equipped, and ready to go.

Now we faced only one potentially serious problem. Another expedition beat us in reserving the south ridge route we had hoped to ski. We would have to try for the north side instead. Unfortunately, our only foreknowledge of that route was gleaned from a postcard, in which a cloud hid the bottom 3,000 feet (1,000 m) of the route.

Tibetan Buddhist lamas pray at Tengboche Monastery, near Mount Everest.

THE HAUNTED TEMPLE

August 21, 1980 (Day 12)

As occurs every monsoon, rains have closed the only airstrip near the Khumbu, so we have hired fifty porters and are trekking the entire 170 miles (285 km) to our base camp. We have already been walking for six days from a trailhead in Lamosangu, with another ten between us and the Dzonglha Valley, where we will set up our climbing school. As we move eastward, every step plods steeply up or down one of six major north–south ridges. In fact, on this hike to the base of Mount Everest we will gain (and lose) more than the mountain's 29,035-foot (8,850 m) elevation.

Down in the canyons we can scarcely hear ourselves above roaring rivers as we wind between verdant terraced fields. Most villagers are friendly, especially when Peter and I greet them in Nepali, and—except for a brief moment when a cobra drops onto the trail in front of us—everything seems bucolic and timeless. And then we climb, climb, and climb, still working eastward, until we enter deserted forests of rhododendrons and azaleas that are hung with creepy moss and shrouded in fog. Locals say that ghosts haunt these places and that it's suicidal to travel here at night. A yeti might attack us, warned one old crone, or perhaps an evil spirit would steal our souls while we slept.

Today we stumbled more than a vertical mile up one of the highest ridges. Just at daybreak we briefly glimpsed Mounts Gauri Shankar and Melungtse, but these were quickly swallowed by clouds. All morning we sweltered under hot, humid sun, and then huge thunderheads boiled out of the Indian plains, zapping down lightning and so much rain that it felt as if fire hoses were trained on our umbrellas.

To our dismay—and especially to our fifty porters'—nightfall catches us with no flat place to camp, and no teahouse, only a tiny temple that will fit two sleeping people. Some time after Jay drifts off, he discovers that a leech has attached to his eyelid and sucked enough blood to swell from the size of a small worm to bigger than his finger. As tough as he is, I know he wants to scream as he sprinkles it with salt to release its tenacious grip. Strange birds and monkeys call from nearby trees and I wonder if the locals are correct about ghosts. As tired as we are, none of us sleeps very well.

SHERPAS IN SPACE

September 18, 1980 (Day 40)

Ang Dale Sherpa teeters atop a huge overhanging rock, noticeably uncomfortable about his life's first rappel. Peter and I try to coax him, and our Sherpa co-instructors, veteran expedition sirdars Pasang Kami and Pertemba, shout encouragement: *"Dar hundana, sarjilo chha!"* "Don't worry, it's easy!" One of his friends has him locked into a solid belay, and Ang Dale

finally relents, backing down into space, where he slowly rotates in the air, grimacing as if he thinks he is going to plummet to his death.

We're well into our third week-long session, each with twelve different students (some of whom have climbed Mount Everest several times), and their response has been overwhelming gratitude—even if it has rained nearly all day, every day. Not once have we seen any adjacent mountain, even though some are almost close enough to touch. Then, like a curtain on a stage, the clouds suddenly part, revealing one tiny section of the panorama that lures so many climbers and trekkers to the Khumbu. I grab my camera, fire away at the remaining rappellers, and revel in long-forgotten sunshine. It's time to go climbing!

RAPTURE OF THE HEIGHTS

October 9, 1980 (Day 61)

Today begins at 18,000-foot (5,500 m) Camp One, way before dawn—an hour at which I am loath to rise. I hear John start the stove at 3 A.M., and I burrow deeper into my sleeping bag, realizing I have scant minutes before I have to emerge into subzero darkness, find my outer garments, lace up my boots, and try to look happy as my shivering hands wrap around a rapidly cooling cup of coffee. I somehow accomplish this more quickly than usual and John comments on my speed.

"My biggest worry before this trip was whether I could get you out of bed early enough," he laughs. Peter chuckles too, and I hear Jay frantically zipping and lacing to catch up—another uncommon occurrence.

With only primitive headlamps for light, the four of us choke down cups of granola and set forth, following wands we had placed earlier to guide us through a maze of hidden crevasses. Eerie seracs loom like ghosts overhead and I worry that one might topple down on us.

We reach the fixed ropes by dawn and John and I start upward, adding extra rope to our packs so that we can push a few hundred feet higher up the face before afternoon storm clouds roll in. This part of the route is far more difficult than we anticipated. We have abandoned any hope of skiing; we will be thrilled just to climb the mountain.

John, the veteran mountain guide, powers up his 200-foot (60 m) pitch. After he sets his anchors, I follow, stringing out thin polypropylene rope that we will use as a fixed line. Next it is my turn to lead and I am intimidated by the strange snow, which has formed a series of parallel ridges called "flutes"—a common feature on steep, snowy mountain walls. These are very scenic from a distance, but fearsome up close because the gullies between the ridges are created by avalanching snow. Whenever possible we climb on the flutes, and when forced to traverse the 20 or 30 feet (6 to 10 m) from one to another, we scamper without delay.

By the time I finish leading my section, it is late in the afternoon, clouds have rolled in, and Jay and Peter have descended after carrying up more ropes and other supplies. John and I tinker for a long time with the anchors, and when at last we complete this, John rappels first. I promise to straighten out the fixed line after he reaches the bottom so that it runs down the tops of the flutes rather than in the gullies. This takes longer than expected.

Being alone in such a vulnerable place frightens me, but by the time I finish placing midpoint anchors the clouds mysteriously dissolve, revealing a panorama

Jay Jensen and a porter on Lamjura Pass, which some locals believe is haunted.

Pertemba Sherpa teaches rappelling during Sherpa climbing courses. Ama Dablam is in the background.

that exceeds my wildest expectations. Suddenly, I am bathed in the kind of light that occurs at what photographers call "the magic hour," but this is beyond anything I have witnessed before. Am I seeing the handiwork of God?

The view stretches my imagination. To my left, just beyond several "minor" 20,000-foot (6,000 m) peaks, is 22,395-foot (6,828 m) Ama Dablam, sacred to the Sherpas and possibly the most beautiful mountain on earth. To my right is Island Peak, my first Himalayan summit, totally overshadowed by the 2-mile high (3,300 m) Lhotse–Nuptse Wall, glowing an otherworldly golden hue. And these are just portals to a heavenly range that stretches more than a thousand miles (1,600 km) farther west, casting long purple shadows that will soon engulf me in numbing cold. A mystical, golden halo encircles the setting sun, sparkling with so many airborne ice crystals that the sky is alive.

I know that I need to hurry down the steep flutes and pay constant attention to avoid snagging my wind pants with my crampons, but I sense an aura all around. At this very second I gain a unique and magnificent perspective on a real, tangible world, with more things to see and more events happening than I could absorb in a thousand lifetimes: a never-ending drama with a stage as big as the massifs themselves. Right in front of me is a microcosm of the world, with action as intense as tectonic geology or as tiny as the icicles dripping beside me; with characters ranging from famous mountaineers to yaks to the tiniest insects buzzing around the villages below. I feel like my mind has shifted onto another plane and everything around me looks slower, clearer, and more perfect than anything I have ever witnessed. How could such a thing ever be created?

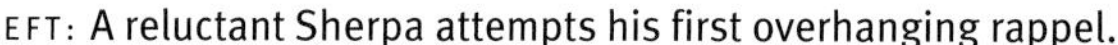

LEFT: A reluctant Sherpa attempts his first overhanging rappel.

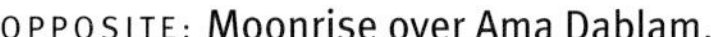

OPPOSITE: Moonrise over Ama Dablam.

By the time I see the highest wands leading back to Camp One my euphoria has faded and I recognize that any spiritual implications of the moment are probably just hallucinations brought on by exhaustion and dehydration, which can always play tricks on your mind. Nevertheless, I will never forget that moment. If nothing else, I, young Gordon Wiltsie, have proved to myself that I can go up on a mountain as imposing as Baruntse, accomplish my share of climbing, photograph the expedition, and do so safely. If I can do this and gradually gain more skills and confidence, who knows what panoramas lie ahead?

BELOW: Peter Hackett climbs a steep snow flute on the northeast face of Baruntse. The Imja Valley and Ama Dablam can be seen in the background.

OPPOSITE: The expedition route up the northeast headwall of Baruntse. Camp Two was on the other side of the North Col (second notch from left), about 100 vertical meters below the ridgeline. When we planned our climb from a postcard, this section was hidden by a cloud.

PERILOUS POWDER

October 14, 1980 (Day 66)

Usually I enjoy leading, being on the "sharp end" of the rope. But now, at about 19,800 feet (6,035 m), the task has lost its charm. After three weeks spent ferrying loads and fixing ropes, we've finally overcome an icy couloir that splits an otherwise impenetrable rock band. Now we are only a couple hundred feet (60 m) below Baruntse's North Col, where we plan to establish Camp Two.

Just a few days ago, before we retreated to base camp to rest for our summit push, Jay thought he was going to die in that couloir. A blizzard engulfed him as he led this ambitious pitch, packing gusts so strong that I couldn't hear his hollers for "SLACK!" His crampons barely penetrated the steep water ice, and he had already placed all of his ice screws far below. Most were barely spiraled into bad snow, and if he fell, he'd most likely rip everything out, plummet 400 feet (120 m), and drag me off the mountain.

In a desperate grope, he found a solitary crack in a rock he could barely reach. He grabbed one of his few pitons, stuffed it into the fissure, and hammered it home. Nowhere else could he find an anchor. "I swear," he told me in agnostic humor after he had fixed the rope and rappelled back down to my belay, "I saw Jesus up there!"

Now I face the opposite problem. Instead of ice, my purchase is near-vertical unconsolidated snow that is barely glued to whatever lies beneath. Neither my crampons nor my ice axes will bite, and with every "step" I sink to my waist. To make any progress, I tunnel with a shovel and grovel on my knees. Except for one piton that I know will not hold, I can place no intermediate anchor.

This has created an awkward situation. Our plan was for Peter and me to hasten up this last pitch and fix a line to the col. John and Jay would dawdle below and then follow us, avoiding congestion and overweighting of Jay's solitary piton. By now, however, both have arrived at Peter's belay station and they're all hanging together as I wallow upward.

Peter Hackett below the cornice on the east side of Baruntse's North Col.

I know that if I fall, everyone else will follow. For what seems like hours I burrow both sideways and upward. I hear plaintive queries about how far I am from the top. Then, just as darkness falls, I pull over a cornice onto the col. For the first time all day the snow is flat. I pound in two pickets and fix a rope that the others can climb with a ratcheting device called a "jumar."

Peter comes first. As he unclips from the anchor and weights the line, my intermediate piton pops loose. I hear a scream as he swings 50 feet (15 m) sideways. He thinks that the top-most anchors have pulled and is certain that he is plummeting to his death. As he rockets into space, Jay turns to John and asks in all seriousness, "Are we going to die?"

By midnight—after John's eyelids had briefly frozen shut—everyone joins me on the col, but we

LEFT: Our team wakes in our frigid open-air bivouac at 20,000 feet (6,100 m) on Baruntse's North Col.

BELOW: Jay Jensen in a snow cave at Camp Two, tired and hungry after a long day.

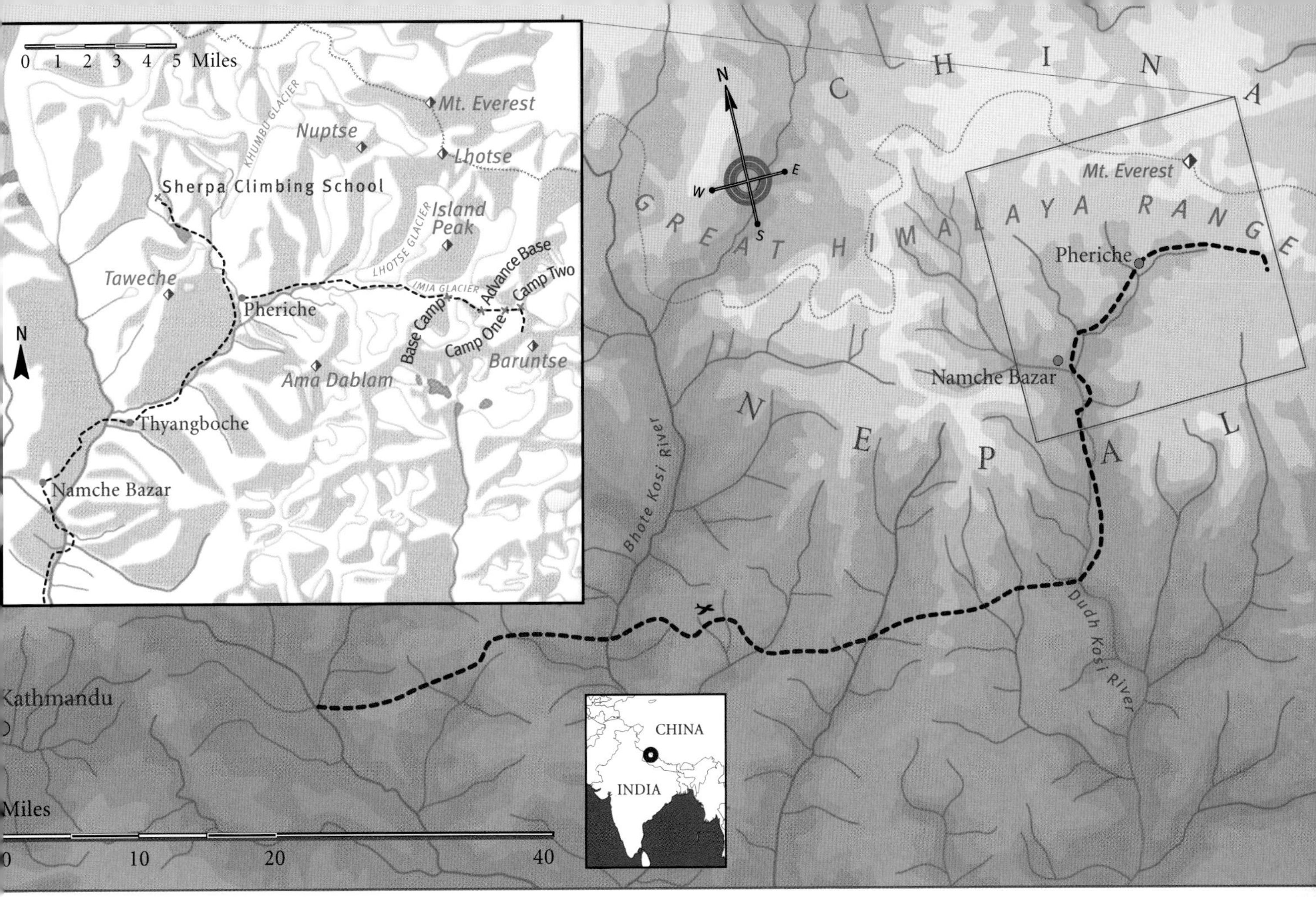

have to search for a bivouac. We are too tired to dig a snow cave and haven't brought a tent, so we sleep in the open as temperatures sink far below zero. At least it isn't windy.

THE JET STREAM

October 17, 1980 (Day 69)

Just as we are approaching Baruntse's 23,005-foot (7,014 m) north summit—which we have now decided is high enough for us—the wind begins to blow. After a pre-dawn start from a snow cave we dug below our initial bivouac on the east side below the col, we've powered up just over 3,000 vertical feet (900 m) to an elevation close to 23,000 feet (7,000 m). We are climbing in teams of two and moments earlier bagging the sub-summit seemed assured. Then, with no warning, the jet stream drops—an annual meteorological event that usually ends the fall climbing season across Nepal. Gusts suddenly exceed 100 mph (165 kph), and the previously slack ropes between us arc horizontally into the air. Spindrift tears at exposed flesh.

I'm at the bottom of our team and see John stop to confer with Jay. Inexplicably, they dig a snow pit and crawl in. As Peter and I catch up, they are stamping their feet and looking forlorn. They say their toes now feel like wood and they worry about proceeding. We share a cigarette, pour a cup of tea from our thermos, and discuss our options. The weather is deteriorating so fast that we know that we have to choose between the summit and our digits, perhaps even our lives. As the last ash sparkles toward adjacent Mount Makalu, we begin our descent.

FOLLOWING SPREAD: Peter Hackett on Baruntse's north ridge. Imja Glacier, Island Peak, and Lhotse are in the background.

FINAL SPREAD IN CHAPTER: Mount Everest on the left, Nuptse on the right. A year after this "training expedition" on Baruntse, Peter Hackett climbed Mount Everest.

CHAPTER TWO

WINGS UNDER THE WORLD

Unlocking the Heart of Antarctica, 1988–1989

- ***Locations:*** Patriot Hills Expedition Base, the Vinson Massif, Polar Plateau, and Calley Glacier on the Antarctic Peninsula
- ***Dates:*** Various trips between January 1988 and December 1989
- ***Conditions:*** Almost always subfreezing and usually below 0°F (–18°C), with weather ranging from clear skies and calm to blizzards with wind speeds of more than 80 mph (135 kph)

UNTIL 1983 THE VAST INTERIOR of earth's southernmost continent was a private preserve—some would even say a paradise—for a few privileged scientists and the technicians who supported their research. Admittedly, Antarctica's shoreline had been violated by Lars Eric Lindblad in 1966 when he began carrying shipboard tourists to the Antarctic Peninsula, but everything beyond was forbidden landscape for those without governmental blessings.

This was not a matter of international law, simply one of accessibility. The only large, ski-equipped aircraft capable of landing on the continent were government owned. Without massive risk and a huge financial investment there was simply no way for private citizens to venture beyond the coast. Then, in the early 1980s, American businessmen Dick Bass and Frank Wells made a pact to become the first people to climb the highest mountain on each of the seven continents. Although Mount Everest was their most daunting physical challenge, Antarctica's 16,067-foot (4,897 m) Vinson Massif was the logistical crux.

This imposing high point of the Ellsworth Mountains, only 788 miles (1,312 km) from the South Pole, had been climbed in 1966 by an expedition sponsored by the National Geographic Society with aviation support from the National Science Foundation (NSF). It had also been climbed in 1979 by a scientific party. Since then, the NSF had refused to support any similar undertakings. Indeed, their official policy was to discourage private explo-

A ski-equipped Twin Otter flies in front of 16,067-foot (4,897 m) Vinson Massif, the highest mountain in Antarctica.

OPPOSITE: Paradise Bay, the place where I first fell in love with Antarctica.

ration on the continent, citing potential rescue costs, environmental damage, and interference with their scientific mission.

As a consequence, Bass and Wells needed to find their own ski plane and pilot. They turned to Giles Kershaw, a former flier for the British Antarctic Survey. Kershaw had buzzed over the continent for years and was awestruck by its beauty. He believed that its long-term ecological survival depended on allowing a broader audience to see it, even if abetting this meant—in some people's eyes—becoming a traitor to his former employer. He found a Douglas DC-3 (a venerable, twin-propeller airliner first built in the 1930s) that had been refurbished into a unique three-engine, ski-equipped Tri-Turbo. Its turbine engines were safer than the old ones driven by pistons and crankshafts, and he believed that it could carry Bass, Wells, and eight other mountaineers (all led by legendary expedition leader Sir Christian Bonington) 1,700 miles (2,700 km) one-way from the tip of South America. And indeed, he and the plane delivered everyone safely to Vinson base camp in November 1983.

In ensuing years, he flew smaller Twin Otter bush planes (also equipped with skis) to ferry numerous other teams to the mountain. In the process, he partnered with Canadian mountain guides Pat Morrow and Martyn Williams, along with other backers, to establish Adventure Network International (ANI), the first private "airline" in Antarctica.

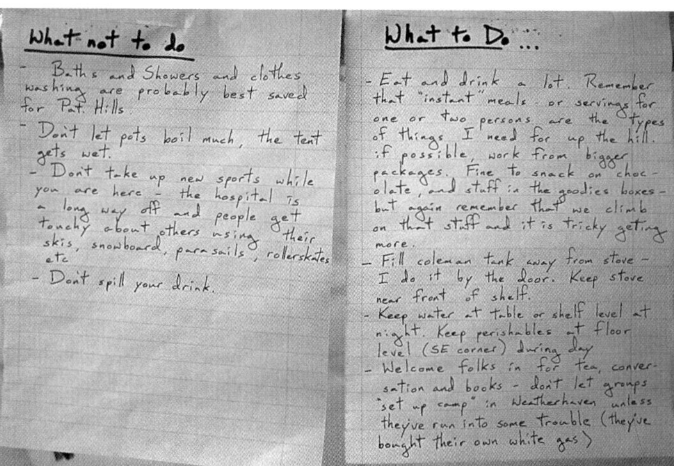

What not to do

- Baths and Showers and clothes washing are probably best saved for Pat. Hills.
- Don't let pots boil much, the tent gets wet.
- Don't take up new sports while you are here - the hospital is a long way off and people get touchy about others using their skis, snowboard, parasails, rollerskates etc
- Don't spill your drink.

What to Do...

- Eat and drink a lot. Remember that "instant" meals or servings for one or two persons are the types of things I need for up the hill. if possible, work from bigger packages. Fine to snack on chocolate, and stuff in the goodies boxes - but again remember that we climb on that stuff and it is tricky getting more.
- Fill coleman tank away from stove - I do it by the door. Keep stove near front of shelf.
- Keep water at table or shelf level at night. Keep perishables at floor level (SE corner) during day
- Welcome folks in for tea, conversation and books - don't let groups "set up camp" in Weatherhaven unless they've run into some trouble (they've bought their own white gas)

TOP TO BOTTOM: Adventure Network guides dig out a wheeled Douglas DC-4 that mired in deep snow after missing the ice runway during landing. Incidents such as this were commonplace in the company's early days.

Notes to guests at Adventure Network's Mount Vinson base camp.

To help preserve Antarctica's uniquely pristine environment, visitors to Mount Vinson base camp are expected to fly out everything they bring in, including their human waste.

A camp hand at Patriot Hills Expedition Base shovels drifting snow during gale winds in 1996. Bad weather is common and can delay flights for weeks.

Dr. Ibrahim Abdulhamid Alam, one of the first two Saudi Arabian tourists to visit the South Pole, as partial sponsors of Will Steger's 1989–1990 Trans-Antarctica Expedition.

Aside from the dangers of flying so far over the world's wildest seas, where wings can ice and winds can blow hard enough to make a plane fly backwards, Kershaw's primary limitation was fuel. Early on, he arranged for a ship to place a large cache on the coast of the Antarctic Peninsula, but even with this, Vinson was as far as he could reach. Giles's dream was to open up the entire continent. The only way to accomplish this was to find a bare ice glacier where incessant katabatic winds blow away the loose snow and ANI could land a large *wheeled* aircraft that was big enough to carry a cargo of fuel. Working with British glaciologist Dr. Charles Swithenbank, he located one at 80° S next to the Patriot Hills, about 100 miles (170 km) southeast of Vinson. From there, ANI could use Twin Otters to shuttle passengers as far as they were able to leap-frog drums of Jet-A. Their first project, they decided, would be to fly the first-ever tourists to the South Pole—at a cost of $35,000 per person.

I learned about Adventure Network in 1987, the first season they began flying a propeller-driven DC-4 to the Patriot Hills. A year earlier I had traveled to the continent on a ship and became so captivated by its majesty that I was desperate to return. I got my chance as a consequence of an article about that cruise that I wrote for *Travel and Leisure* magazine. Because this helped Leo LeBon, the founder of Mountain Travel (for which Meredith and I had worked as Himalayan guides) sell out a chartered polar cruise, he rewarded me with an invitation to join him on a climb of Mount Vinson. For complex reasons that expedition evaporated, but I nevertheless proceeded to Punta Arenas, Chile, and introduced myself to Martyn Williams.

After proving my willingness to do almost anything to help, he invited me to be a camp hand at the expedition base they had established at Patriot Hills. Thus began an unexpected chapter in my life that would lead to eleven Antarctic journeys and nearly as many to the Arctic.

EMPTINESS

Early January 1988

■ ***Location:*** Patriot Hills Expedition Base; 80° S, 79° W; 690 miles (1,150 km) north of the South Pole and approximately 1,600 miles (2,700 km) south of Cape Horn

For the first time in my life, I feel utterly alone. I ski beyond the tents at Patriot Hills toward the Three Sails, a trio of small nunataks, the tops of mountains otherwise buried in a glacier. After I crest a small rise, the camp disappears from sight. On three sides the horizon seems as flat as an ocean, and my skis glide up and over endless, wind-sculpted waves, *sastrugi.* Except for gentle hissing of snow crystals in a light, subzero wind, my own breathing is the solitary sound and I can see nothing man made. Only the hills behind lend any sense that this place is set on earth. The emptiness of this landscape is both magnificent and frightening. I can understand how it either inspired or crushed the spirits of so many early explorers.

A few days ago I flew here from Punta Arenas with the first tourists to the South Pole. The plane was a frightening old hulk that had seen better decades, and before taking off, my first job was to clean the evidence of years of oil leaks off the wings so it wouldn't frighten passengers more accustomed to flying first class on Air France. The subsequent ten-hour flight itself was not particularly terrifying, but I couldn't help remembering stories about an earlier flight that season (the second one ever made to Patriot Hills). On that journey, the DC-4 weather-cocked in a side wind after touching down and spun 180 degrees on the ice, rocketing straight for the hills at 80 mph (135 kph), tail first. Only brilliant piloting saved the day. Fortunately, our landing was less eventful, although still frightening when the plane banged and bounced onto the glacier with deafening noise.

Unlike many of my fellow passengers, who had come primarily for bragging rights about having "bagged" the pole, I was instantly bewitched by the Antarctic interior. I loved the lonely tent camp and was baffled when my companions began complaining

Adventure Network's Patriot Hills Expedition Base, 1988.

Chilean mountaineer Alejo Contreras Staeding tries to parasail the katabatic winds on the sastrugi-carved Polar Plateau near Patriot Hills Expedition Base. The Three Sails nunataks can be seen in the distance.

about almost everything, especially the weather that kept them from flying immediately onward to the pole. Most couldn't wait to get home.

I was especially shocked to overhear arguments from several competitive travelers who kept checklists of every place they had ever entered a transit lounge. Many were angry to learn that the pie-slice-shaped part of Antarctica that Norway claims does not actually reach the pole. As a consequence, when they tiptoed around the ceremonial barber pole at 90° S, they would only be able to tick off the pole and the other six claims that meet there. Norway's territory—which includes Queen Maud Land—remained beyond their reach. Despite all the beauty around us, some felt cheated.

I didn't care that there was no space on the Twin Otters for me to join the group headed toward the pole. I was happy enough to explore the immediate, largely unknown vicinity, either alone or with my fellow guides and camp hands. Each "evening" (the sun never set), after a long "day" of feeding and entertaining our two dozen or so guests, we would venture forth. Sometimes we made first ascents of nearby peaks, gazing from perspectives no human had ever seen before. Other times, like now, I set off alone, reveling in the solitude and emptiness that can be found few other places on earth. I am badly bitten by what some call the "polar bug."

ROOF OF THE CONTINENT

December 11, 1988

- ***Location:*** 15,292-foot (4,661 m) Mount Shinn, Antarctica's third highest mountain; 78° S, 86° W; in the Sentinel Range of the Ellsworth Mountains, approximately 800 miles (1,333 km) north of the South Pole
- ***Members:*** Adventure travel pioneer Mike McDowell, veteran New Zealand photographer and polar explorer Colin Monteath, Australian mountaineer Greg Mortimer, Dr. Lis Densmore from the Yukon, and Gordon Wiltsie

I wake around nine, grateful that bad weather has not sneaked up on our dangerously vulnerable high camp in a 12,500-foot (3,800 m) col between the summits of Mounts Vinson and Shinn. Fortunately, several of my companions are veteran Antarctic mountaineers and we have done everything possible to protect our tents from hurricane-force winds that can spring from nowhere. We built thick, meter-high walls of snow blocks all around us and lashed down each tent with a spiderweb of climbing ropes attached to a dozen ice screws. Nevertheless, even that could fail if Antarctica shows us the worst that she can deliver.

Two days ago everyone in our group climbed Mount Vinson, including Lis, who became the first woman to ascend the peak. Yesterday we rested outside our tents in weather that seemed balmy, and today all of us except Lis plan to try Mount Shinn. Oddly, we don't feel rushed, because the sun's elevation never changes much as it circles overhead. I gradually unzip my 8-inch-thick (20 cm) sleeping bag—in which I slept fully clothed—and wriggle far enough out to start the stove.

Mike and I plan to climb the standard route, while Colin and Greg will attempt a more difficult new one. We leave around noon, roped up as a precaution against hidden crevasses. As Mike and I climb, we find our route easy but also exhilarating—far more interesting than Mount Vinson, where distant views were hidden first by ridges and then on the summit by ice haze and high clouds. Today the skies are ultra-violet blue and the vistas seem both more immediate and farther reaching. Just north are Mount Epperly, unclimbed, and difficult, craggy Mount Tyree, second-highest peak on the continent, climbed only once. Beyond them march a succession of shapely peaks, some unnamed and almost all untouched.

Even more awesome than the mountain panorama, however, is our aerie-like view of the vast polar cap, where ice up to 3 miles (5 km) thick traps 75 percent of the earth's fresh water and stretches so far to the east and south that it seems as if we can see the planet's curvature. We spiral clockwise up the mountain, and our route suddenly veers up a steep snow ridge leading straight to the summit. Cornices on the west overhang a fearsome drop 6,500 feet (2,000 m) to the glaciers below. By 4:30 P.M., we reach the top and gaze out over a seldom-seen side of the Ellsworth Mountains to the Ronne Ice Shelf and frozen Weddell Sea.

Dr. Lis Densmore, the first woman to climb Mount Vinson, builds snow walls to protect her tent from potential hurricane-force winds. The team also lashed their shelters down with ropes and ice screws.

Mountaineer Hector MacKenzie on a bare-ice glacier near the Patriot Hills. Mount Fordell is in the background.

Despite temperatures that hover somewhere around –25°F (–30°C) and a light wind that adds to the chill, we are too captivated to descend and instead wait for Colin and Greg, who arrive about an hour later, their faces completely rimed and fingers frostbitten from climbing in the shade. Even they disregard the cold, however, and we rejoice atop one of the grandest mountains I have ever climbed.

AN OCEAN OF ICE

December 21, 1988

- ***Location:*** A visually indistinguishable location on the polar ice cap, approximately 84° S, 80° W; about 75 miles north of the Thiel Mountains and 415 miles (690 km) north of the South Pole
- ***Members:*** Co-leaders Martyn Williams and Jim Williams; snowmobile drivers Mike Sharp, a former logistical coordinator at Britain's Rothera science base, and Stuart Hamilton, a hydrologist from the Yukon; and Antarctic veteran Alejo Contreras Staeding, representing the Chilean government. The ski team included Shirley Metz, an entrepreneur from Laguna Beach, California; Jerry Corr, a real estate developer from Lansing, Michigan; Colonel J. K. Bajaj, principal of the mountaineering school in Uttarkashi, India; Ronald Milnarik, a retired air force colonel and endodontist from Belleville, Illinois; Victoria Murden, a graduate student at Harvard Divinity School; and Joseph Murphy, a mountaineer, writer, and retired banker from Minneapolis, Minnesota.

While my companions and I were climbing on Mount Vinson, another hardy group was cross-country skiing across the immense polar ice cap toward the South Pole. It was the first-ever guided trip of this nature, comprised of three leaders, two snowmobile drivers, and six other participants who had each paid approximately $70,000. Two women in the group hoped to be the first of their gender to reach the pole by nonmechanical means.

OPPOSITE: Mike McDowell atop sub-summit of 15,292-foot (4,661 m) Mount Shinn

FOLLOWING SPREAD: The South Pole ski expedition's windswept camp is dwarfed by a vast expanse of snow that is featureless except for endless waves of sastrugi.

Mike Sharp navigates with a sextant.

Now they are running low on food and pilot Henri Perk needs to resupply them. In addition to my duties as camp hand I am also on a test assignment, shooting a few pictures for an upcoming *National Geographic* story on Antarctica, so Henri lets me join him in the copilot's seat. Also aboard are another food cache and several drums of fuel that we will leave near the Thiel Mountains. (By the time the fuel is deposited, the cost of getting it that far will be about $120 a gallon—more expensive than many fine whiskies.)

After Henri expertly gets us airborne, we leave behind any mountains and begin flying across the seemingly infinite polar plateau. Normally the 275-mile (460 km) journey to the group would take him about two hours and 200 gallons (400 l) of fuel. Today, however, we face a low-level katabatic headwind that Henri estimates to be about 60 mph (100 kph), which will cut our ground speed almost in half if we don't climb above it (which we do). At least the gusts will make our plane a racehorse on the return.

We drone along without seeing a single landmark breaking the 360-degree horizon of white. When Henri's sun compass, our most reliable navigation tool, finally tells us we are at the same latitude that Martyn's sextant reports, we radio the group and start looking. I figure it will be easy to spot seven tents and two big snowmobiles. Not so. For almost half an hour we fly back and forth, traversing a huge grid, all the while listening to Martyn become more and more

Jerry Corr heads to his tent in the group's windy camp on the polar plateau.

agitated. Partly he's worried about starving if we can't find them, and as an owner of ANI, he's also worried about all the fuel we're burning.

Finally, just as my own eyes are beginning to feel snow-blinded, Henri says, "There they are!" He banks sharply left as I stare in vain. When at last I see the camp, it seems as tiny as a pinhead held across a room. I gasp at the scale of the landscape the skiers are traversing.

After an astonishingly smooth landing into the wind, the entire group greets us with bear hugs and hastens us into their industrial-strength cook tent, where Jim Williams serves us cocoa and everyone talks at once. Communication is difficult, however, because all of the tents are snapping like gunfire in the wind.

By now the group has been on the trail for seventeen days, and they are looking haggard. I wonder if they can hold out for the remaining forty they estimate they will need to reach the pole. Even with snowmobile support, their routine is brutal, as I learned when I joined them for two days at the very start. All day, every day, subzero katabatic winds pound their faces and freeze snot into icicles. Equally numbing, once they'd left behind the Ellsworths, there was little to see but an infinite white panorama and endless waves of sastrugi, some so high they had to fight to drag even the lightest sleds across. I tell myself that I will be awestruck if they make it to the Pole.

Mike Farny takes a snow bath on the Calley Glacier.

PUSHING THE EXTREMES

December 12, 1989

- ***Location:*** The Calley Glacier on the Antarctic Peninsula; 64° S, 61° W; approximately 1,800 miles (3,000 km) north of the South Pole and 600 miles (1,000 km) south of Cape Horn.
- ***Members:*** Leader Gordon Wiltsie, camp manager David Ostergren, pilot Henri Perk, Warren Miller Ski Films camera crew Brian Sisselman and Bill Heath, and skiing stars Tom Day, Willi Vogl, Kevin Andrews, and Mike Farny.

As I watch Mike Farny front-point around an icy crevasse on the steep slopes of Mount Berry, I feel deeply conflicted. His goal is to help cameraman Brian Sisselman obtain spectacular footage: Mike will climb above this yawning maw, make two turns, and then leap over it.

The photographer part of me exults. "Extreme" is the byword of the times and my official job is to help Brian and this team of elite skiers return home with the most extreme footage they can possibly film at one of the most extreme locations on earth. We've already climbed a first ascent, used the Twin Otter for "heli-skiing," and even faked a death-defying blizzard using the prop-wash of the plane. At least this is real. "Jump!" I think.

Extreme skier Mike Farny above a serac on Mount Berry.

On the other hand, I am also the guide, hired to keep everyone safe. If Mike slips on the ice or doesn't hit his takeoff perfectly, he could easily disappear into the crevasse and fall so far we would never see him again. Even if he only breaks his leg, the nearest hospital is at least 700 miles (1,150 km) away, and weather safe enough for flying is never assumed. A year earlier a group I was leading nearby had been stuck in a storm for ten days before our veteran pilot dared take off. Teams of scientists have been stuck a month or more. "Are you out of your mind to allow this?" the saner part of me counters.

Ultimately I say nothing, Mike jumps, and both Brian and I shoot incredible footage. As has happened many times in my life, I've once again escaped disaster.

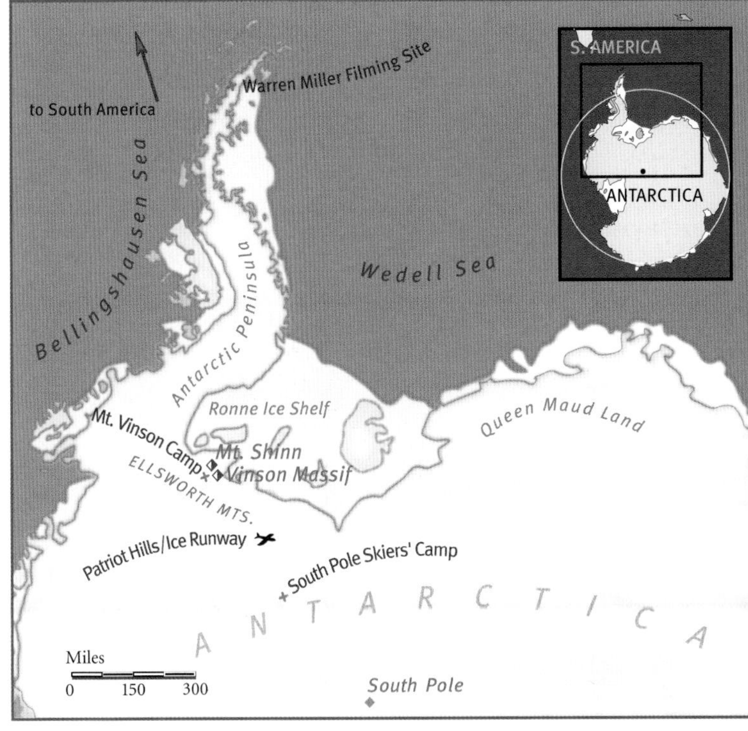

Mike Farny jumars up a serac en route to attempting a big jump for the expedition camera crew.

Ski mountaineer Tom Day crosses the Calley Glacier in front of a dramatic summit I mistakenly thought was Pilcher Peak. Later an Australian expedition attempted it, based on this picture, and discovered I had captioned it mistakenly. They named it "Wiltsie's Peak" to commemorate my error.

Achilles
15

CHAPTER THREE

MOUNTAINS OF FOG AND FURY

Traversing Terra Incognita, Cordillera Sarmiento, Chile, 1992

- ***Location:*** The southern Chilean fjords; 52° S, 73° W; approximately 45 miles (70 km) west-southwest of Puerto Natales and 20 miles (30 km) due south of the Southern Patagonian Ice Cap
- ***Team:*** Jack Miller (leader), Rob Hart, Tyler Van Arsdell, Peter Garber, Phillip Lloyd, and Gordon Wiltsie
- ***Dates:*** August 16 to October 1, 1992, not including travel time to or from the United States or prep time in Puerto Natales, Chile
- ***Conditions:*** Generally miserable with rain, snow, and winds exceeding 100 mph (165 kph). Temperatures seldom registered much higher or lower than freezing, and out of forty-seven days in the field only five could be deemed "nice." We were never dry.

PATAGONIA'S MINARET-SHAPED MOUNTAINS and maze-like fjords generate some of the world's foulest weather. Tempestuous storms from the Roaring Forties and Furious Fifties swirl unabated across the Pacific, then slam into the southern Andes, pounding them with winds in excess of 100 mph (165 km) and torrential rain or snow. Climbers tread the region in fear.

Expedition leader Jack Miller studies a crude map of Cordillera Sarmiento in the galley of motorsailer *Trinidad*.

Although some Patagonia ranges, including the Torres del Paine and the Fitzroy Massif, boast breathtaking granite spires and attract hundreds of daring alpinists each year, nearby regions remain virtually unexplored. Prominent among these is the Cordillera Sarmiento, the southernmost finger of the continental Andes, which lies slightly west of Patagonia proper and catches the fullest brunt of austral weather. It is so often shrouded in clouds that even by 1977 it hadn't been photographed well enough by satellites for NASA to map it. At that time there was no mention in any alpine journal of anyone going there.

OPPOSITE: Jack Miller and Phillip Lloyd under the calving face of an icefall near base camp.

Rob Hart secures a load on *Trinidad* during heavy seas.

ABOVE RIGHT: Rob Hart explores the boggy terrain.

RIGHT: Phillip Lloyd rides in a motorized raft in heavy seas. The glacier ice at his feet is for refrigerating our food back at camp.

This mystery fascinated Jack Miller, an adventure travel pioneer who knew Patagonia's hidden byways as well as anyone. He first sighted the Sarmiento in 1974 from a summit 80 miles (130 km) away, and returned three years later with his friend Dan Asay to check it out. They camped on the shore under incessant clouds for three sodden weeks but never saw a clear panorama. Finally they stumbled up to a summit they could neither see nor identify, and subsequently retreated.

Then, in February 1990, while leading a tour, Jack again spotted the range from a distant highway. He quickly chartered a plane and witnessed "a massif that would rank in scale with the French Alps or large parts of Alaska's Coastal Range." With him was Rob Hart, the inventor of a popular outdoor camping chair, and together they conspired to mount an expedition not only to climb some of the Sarmiento's highest peaks, but also to investigate its flora and fauna and to obtain newfangled global positioning data to begin mapping the area. I had recently befriended Rob while shooting a magazine story in Montana; in 1975 Jack had been the first person to hire me as a mountain guide. Because they knew I was a prominent photographer who might help them to find sponsorship, they invited me to join them.

To round out the team, Jack invited two of his local climbing buddies from Telluride, Colorado: Peter Garber, who otherwise worked as a carpenter, and Tyler Van Arsdell, a former New England fisherman who was building houses to save money for architecture school. Finally, he invited Phillip Lloyd, a young South African climbing star he had met in Patagonia while Phillip was on an extended sabbatical from law school.

As with any expedition, funding was our first major obstacle. To our delight, we applied for a prestigious Shipton-Tilman grant from W. L. Gore and Associates, makers of Gore-Tex, and were awarded $11,000. We also sent a story proposal to *National Geographic,* where several editors were intrigued by the large blank spot on the map (less so by what they called our "pseudo science"). They gave us seed money and a speculative assignment. Finally, the North American marketing director for Ladeco Airlines figured that any publicity about southern Chile would help them to sell tickets to tourists, and gave us free airfare. Sponsorship in kind from several outdoor equipment companies got us clothed and equipped, and we had everything we needed to depart.

August 17, 1992 (Day 2)

While steaming up remote Fjord of the Mountains in the motorsailer *Trinidad,* I am captivated by the fogbound landscape. Beautiful, weather-beaten beech trees cling to cliffs and resemble bonsai gardens. Periodically we see precipitous icefalls tumbling down from glaciers lost in the clouds. The fjord itself is scarcely a mile wide (2 km) and stretches like a pointed finger 35 miles (60 km) due north. After churning for several hours straight toward the mysterious Southern Patagonian Ice Cap, we finally spot a site that might be flat enough to pitch our *camp.* We go ashore.

Instantly, we learn that travel is going to be difficult here. Two steps inland, and we are pushing aside thorny branches and squishing into bottomless, soggy moss. Suddenly Rob drops to his chest in a hidden pit of icy water. "We're going to *camp* in this bloody bog?" he moans.

We intentionally came in winter, hoping that snow would cover this problematic ground. But no snow was to be seen. Fortunately, Jack had anticipated this contingency and brought along lumber and plywood from which we can construct a deck for our cooking and storage tent. I pitch my own tent atop several bushes that although lumpy promise to keep me dry. Others find niches on rocky ledges above, reachable only by semi-serious climbing that could prove tricky in the dark. Rain starts gushing from the sky, and we start to think it's going to be a long, soggy couple of months.

NEAR-DROWNING

August 19, 1992 (Day 4)

The *Trinidad* departed yesterday, motoring about 70 miles (115 km) back to Puerto Natales. Now we're alone in one of earth's wildest places, connecting to the outside world only by once-a-week radio calls.

Miraculously, clouds parted this morning and we finally glimpse our spectacular setting. Jack enthusiastically launches our little motorized raft for a tour. Phillip and I clamber in after him. We motor into a nearby L-shaped bay filled with ice chunks and walled on three sides by towering cliffs and two massive icefalls that tumble down from an ice cap at least 3,000 feet (1,000 m) above. The landscape is haunting, and I scramble onto a small rock island to shoot my companions cruising through it.

After firing a few frames, however, I hear an ominous crraack. I yell for them to flee and moments later a 100-foot-tall (30 m) serac collapses into the bay. For a split second I am exhilarated, but then a massive wave—taller than my rock—rebounds. Jack and Phillip float harmlessly over it, but as I brace myself (cursing at having forgotten my life jacket), it explodes over my head. Miraculously, I am not washed into the sea; my boots and cameras would have dragged me to the bottom. I emerge soaked, but unharmed. My rock is now covered in huge ice blocks, any one of which could have smashed me senseless.

August 30, 1992 (Day 15)

After eleven miserable days of often-fruitless route-finding, staggering under 80 pound (35 kg) packs, we have established both an advance base camp as well as a higher one just below the higher peaks. Now I'm sitting next to Jack under cobalt skies atop a mountain he calls South Face, which is about 6,000 feet (1,830 m) high and probably the Sarmiento's second tallest peak. The view, which stretches over otherworldly mountains for hundreds of miles, mutes all of our pain. Meanwhile, we're watching another astonishing nearby summit (Jack calls it Gremlin's Cap), as we wait for the rest of our team to climb it for a long-shot photo opportunity. To my relief, condensation that had frozen onto my telephoto's deepest glass thaws just as they reach the base. For more than an hour I shoot at least a dozen rolls of film, whooping in delight. This, I sense, might finally be my "breakthrough picture" for *National Geographic.*

All afternoon we climb other peaks (a total of six), and after retreating to our hard-won high camp—set in a snowy wind scoop, 4,000 feet (1,200 m) above the sea—all are elated. This single day is the reason we came to Chile.

Jack Miller in a raging storm prior to our retreat from high camp.

FOLLOWING SPREAD: Cordillera Sarmiento Expedition members ascend Gremlin's Cap, one of the higher peaks in this previously unexplored range above fjords in southern Chile.

BLOWN AWAY

September 2, 1992 (Day 18)

"Jack, you're being STUPID!" snaps Rob. "You can't go down in weather like this!" Outside our snow cave, gusts are blowing with hurricane force and I can barely stand, much less see through boiling spindrift. Nevertheless, we are running out of food and someone has to return to base to fetch more, as well as to radio Pete's father (our liaison in Puerto Natales) to report that we're still okay. Jack and Pete tried to leave yesterday, but were stopped when Pete, our sturdiest climber, was lifted into the air and blown 30 feet (10 m) uphill.

Although conditions have not improved, Jack now feels even more compelled to get more food and to make his radio call. I agree to join them. Jack yanks out the last stake anchoring our solitary tent, which with my departure is no longer needed. Unfortunately, we didn't first remove all of the support wands that make it a free-standing dome—a veritable parachute. Instantly the wind grabs it and it's gone. Now we *have* to retreat.

First we have to regain the ridge we had climbed from the sea. Once there, the weather's full fury engulfs us. No matter how I shuffle my feet, I can barely stand. Then a gust flattens me, pinning me under my heavy pack. I try to crawl.

"No way!" Jack finally shouts, his words swallowed in a gust. We stagger back down to rejoin Tyler, Phillip, and Rob at the snow cave, where we arrive soaked, facing a life-threatening housing shortage. Everyone scurries to enlarge our bivouac and soon we're all drenched. Worse, Phillip, who had limited snow-camping experience, had dug the entrance down, rather than the more accepted practice of digging up. As a consequence, spindrift clogs our doorway tunnel and breathing hole. Every two hours someone has to crawl out of his sleeping bag, go outside, and re-soak himself shoveling it open again. Heightening my own trauma, I've foolishly brought a goose-down bag up from base camp, rather than my synthetic one. Down would have been fine in the subfreezing temperatures I expected, but this storm has brought a deadly 33°F (1°C) "heat wave" that causes constant dripping (and settling) from the roof. Inside the cave, nothing freezes and nothing dries. By now my bag's feathers have collapsed and I have no insulation except for my sodden clothes. And we're hungry. For dinner, the six of us share two PowerBars, a single serving of freeze-dried eggs, and tea from thrice-used bags.

Our first high camp, before the storm. Later the tent blew away and we had to enlarge the small snow cave to its left.

RETREAT

September 4, 1992 (Day 20)

After a long, cold night, we *all* want to go down. We convince each other that the wind has dropped, even if it hasn't, and somehow find our packs, which had become buried outside under 3 feet (1 m) of new snow. Conditions are at least as bad as before, but this time we forge downward, sometimes on hands and knees. I try skiing, but my fingers are so cold that Phillip has to help me with my bindings. I'm mad; my precious 20 mm lens has frozen at f/2.8. I know that pictures from horrific moments like this can make or break my coverage, so I set the shutter at 1/4,000th of a second and pray that I won't overexpose in the whiteout.

Phillip Lloyd eats his rationed share of instant eggs as Tyler Van Arsdell tries to nap in the snow cave.

At times some of us become separated from the others and we all worry about wandering too far south, where a cliff plummets unknown distances. Below the snow line, our descent gets even trickier, with long, slippery rock slabs separated by thickets of barely penetrable *machai* that scratch our skin and snare the skis that are now tied to our packs. As I struggle, my sodden pants creep down my thighs and begin to hobble me, but my pack is too heavy to set down so that I can pull them back up. I slip down a muddy chute and get hopelessly tangled in a thorn bush below a waterfall. Not caring whether anyone hears or not, I scream with rage and frustration.

Six hours after leaving the snow cave, we finally reach the stony beach where we'd left our raft, but our troubles aren't over. The fjord funnels the wind, producing a seething cauldron of 3-foot-high (1 m) rollers, topped by whitecaps that are themselves whipped into horizontal spray by roaring williwaws. Although it seems dangerous to launch our tiny craft, Jack insists that we have to reach base camp and make our radio call. By now everyone is willing to take a chance (dry clothes and whiskey are cached at the other end), but only three can fit. Jack picks Tyler and me and we set off, promising to come right back for the others—who otherwise will be stranded with only a broken tent and a few food scraps.

Both Tyler and I question Jack's decision to launch, but his skillful helmsmanship keeps us afloat despite waves that crash over the bow, nearly swamp us, and ruin all camera equipment that doesn't encircle my neck. While Tyler bails desperately with a climbing helmet, I avoid panic by shooting pictures. Where, I wonder, am I going to swim when we capsize?

A SECRET LAKE

September 11, 1992 (Day 27)

The *Trinidad* retrieved us two days ago and we have explored the Sarmiento's southern and western shores. Remarkably, the weather has been good and we are awestruck by sea-to-sky panoramas. The range is shaped like a left-facing fishhook, and as we motor into its interior, Taraba Sound, we enter territory that few but local fishermen have ever explored.

After weathering an evening squall in an island's lee, we cruise into a "sub-fjord" beneath the same peaks we climbed on August 30. At last we see

Moss growing beside Taraba Sound. Cordillera Sarmiento is in the far right background.

a hidden route to the range's highest summit and we swarm ashore, scrambling over slippery rock to get a closer view. After hiking about an hour, we glimpse an exquisite lake that we are certain no one has ever seen before—smack in the center in a vast wilderness of *machai*, mossy swamps, cliffs, and tumbling icefalls that guarantee that we're not going to hike to it from here. We agree that this should be a national, or international, park.

THE ENCHANTED FOREST

September 12, 1992 (Day 28)

Trinidad departed this morning, but we are practiced at settling in this particular place we've dubbed Bog Camp II. A unique, rime-coated spire above us resembles a closed fist with middle finger extended. It's as impressive as anything else we've seen in the Cordillera Sarmiento, and we name it the Fickle Finger of Fate. As several of us begin to construct another deck for our communal tent, Rob bursts out of the woods. "You've got to see! I found an enchanted forest!"

He's right. Everything inland resembles a fairy world. Fungi grow on lichens that feed off tree trunks that have somehow anchored themselves in mossy groundcover that seems like a sponge to us human intruders. This place is a cacophony of life force, even if it sometimes seems hell-bent on swallowing us.

OPPOSITE: A glacier empties into a lake below the highest massif of Cordillera Sarmiento.

FOLLOWING SPREAD: The Fickle Finger of Fate.

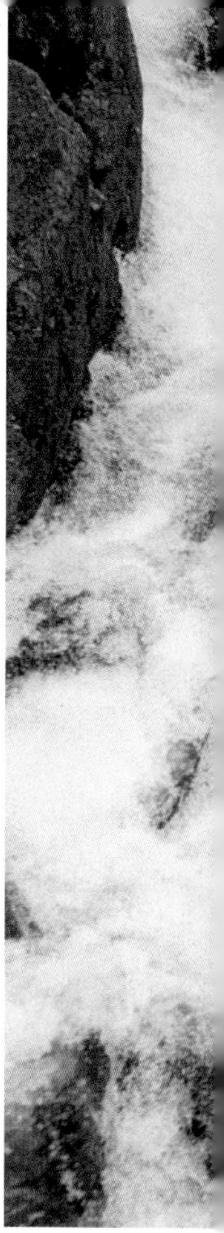

Phillip Lloyd front-points up steep, Styrofoam-textured ice on the Fickle Finger of Fate.

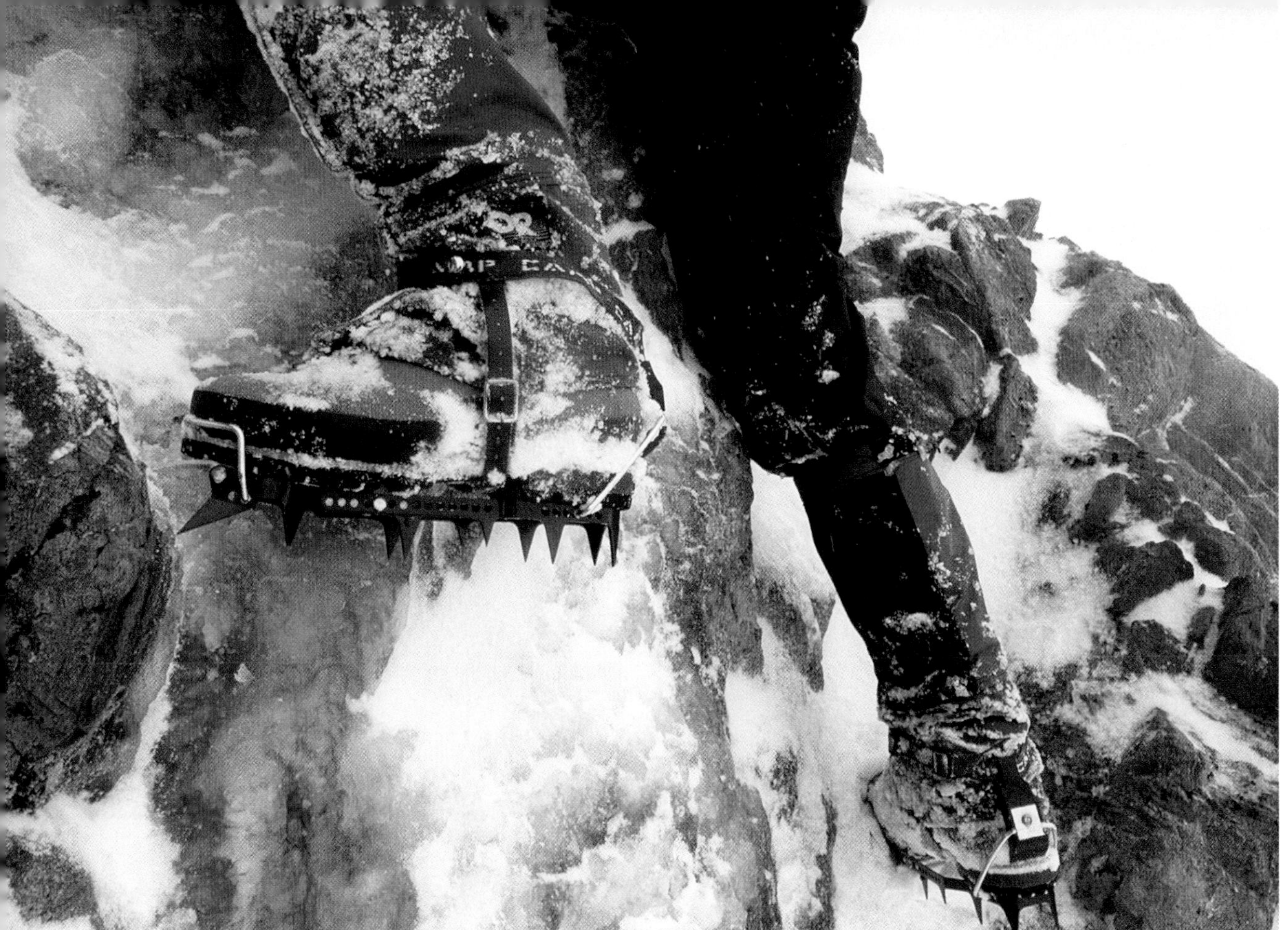

Pete Garber crampons on mixed terrain.

September 15, 1992 (Day 31)

Phillip bellows to wake us at 5:15 A.M. The sky is strewn with stars. We have already hacked a route to the bottom of the Fickle Finger through hideous underbrush, which included a long, slippery log that has fortuitously fallen across a torrent we cannot ford. After thrashing through with skis on our packs, we reach a glacier.

Again, the chance for a day like this is why I came to Chile. The weather is perfect and every step brings broadening panoramas and new technical challenges. I love feeling my crampons crunch into snow that seems like Styrofoam and I can scarcely load film quickly enough to keep up with the group.

Among numerous potential cruxes, the worst is the final digit. From a distance this icy spire looks innocent enough, but once Phillip starts leading, he discovers that it is buried in unconsolidated rime that will hold neither an ice axe nor any form of protection. Nevertheless, he forges far enough above his belayer, Pete, that should he fall, their mutual doom is assured. The rest of us untie from anything connected to them.

Barely 50 feet (15 m) from the summit, Phillip can't go up and for awhile he can't go down. We think he's stranded, but he finally jams in four or five trashy snow pickets that somehow hold as Peter lowers him. We flee to base camp, where we try to dry clothes around a campfire that takes more kerosene than wood to stay lit.

Expedition members kill seemingly endless storm-bound time by fishing in Taraba Sound.

A LONG, WET WAIT

September 30, 1992 (Day 46)

"Miserable" is the keyword for our last two weeks. It has rained or snowed the entire time. At least when I awake and hear the former, I can snuggle in for more sleep. But snow is sneaky and silent. When I stick my head outside to check the weather, I invariably get a neck full of slush that slid off the tent's fly.

We do anything to entertain ourselves: play hearts or cribbage, dry clothes over a gas heater that *Trinidad* brought, or fish in the fjord. Out in the raft, we all hope to catch a big one, but our only prizes seem prehistoric, possibly endangered, and infested with worms. We eat them anyway.

By now, repetition is wearying. There are more snow caves, relentless winds, and less enthusiasm. Three days ago Jack called and asked the *Trinidad* to retrieve us. We wait, and Phillip keeps looking at the peak, thinking that it is mocking us. We hear that the boat is trapped in a bay by williwaws and Phillip nudges Pete. "Let's go for a walk," he suggests. While the rest of us disassemble camp, we follow their

Tyler Van Arsdell with his strangest catch. No one could identify the fish, but we ate it anyway.

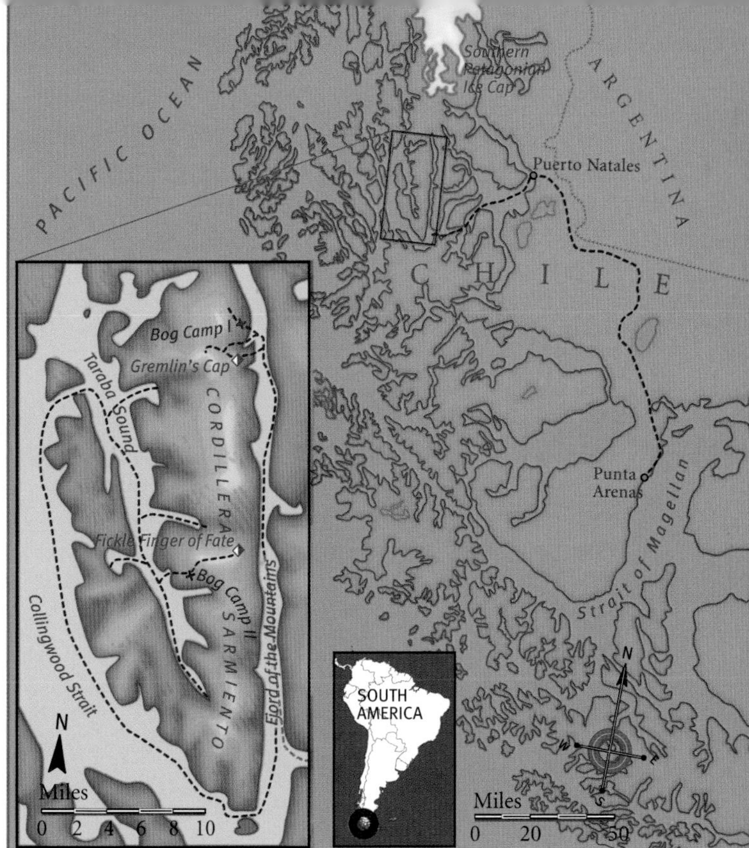

progress though the one set of binoculars that hasn't been ruined by salt spray. Late in the afternoon, a tiny figure emerges atop the Fickle Finger, then two. After sneaking up a different route, they have snatched victory from the winds of Patagonia.*

A few hours later, we swamp our raft twice while ferrying everything out to the *Trinidad.* Pete tumbles into icy seas, followed by Phillip, and it seems an eternity passes before we secure the last load. But there is rum aboard. When Tyler later says that we're speaking Martian, Rob counters that we deserve it.

* Just a year later, Phillip was tragically killed while rappelling in a storm off the legendary Torres del Paine.

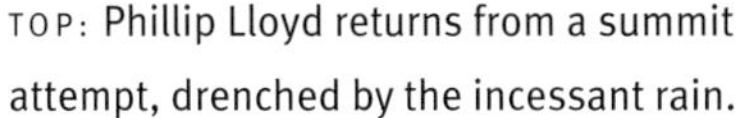

TOP: Phillip Lloyd returns from a summit attempt, drenched by the incessant rain.

MIDDLE: Pete Garber and Phillip Lloyd playing chess, storm-bound, in base camp.

RIGHT: Pete Garber drags the raft after it swamped in gale-force williwaws.

Norman Vaughan stands in front of his mountain.

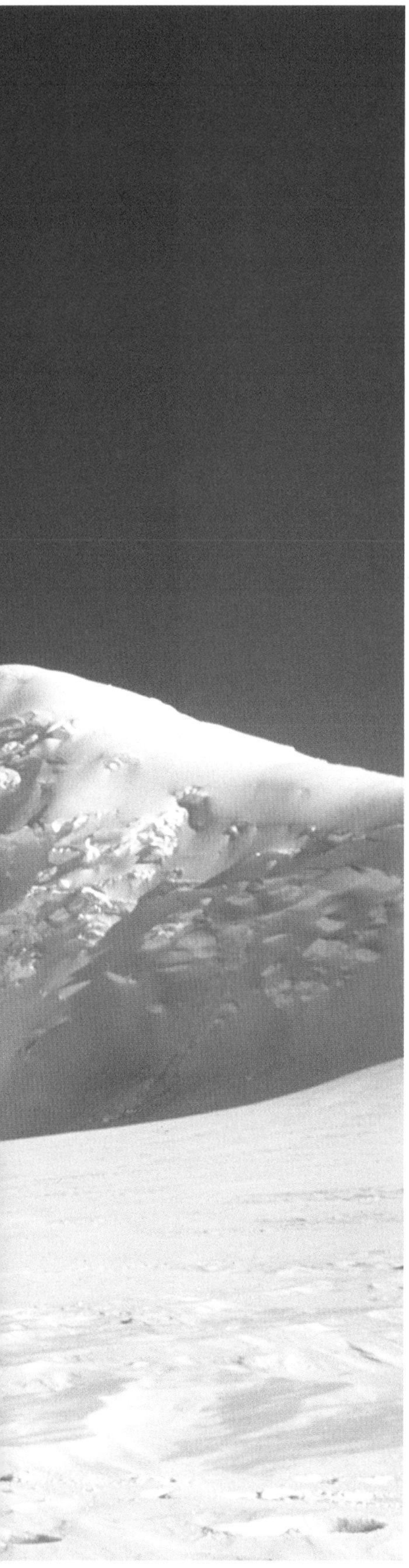

CHAPTER FOUR

THE OLD MAN AND HIS MOUNTAIN

An Octogenarian Revisits the Trans-Antarctic Mountains, 1994

- ***Location:*** Mount Vaughan; 86° S, 156° W; 278 miles (465 km) north of the South Pole in the Queen Maud Mountains, a subrange of the Trans-Antarctic Mountains (not to be confused with Queen Maud Land, which is on the opposite side of the continent)
- ***Team:*** Norman Vaughan, Carolyn Muegge-Vaughan, and Vern Tejas (the Vaughans' personal guide); Gordon Wiltsie (expedition leader) and Rob Hart (assistant leader); Bob Failing and Barry Berkus (expedition supporters); and a *National Geographic* film crew: Larry Engel and Peter Miller, guided by Alejo Contreras Staeding
- ***Dates:*** November 25 to December 20, 1994, from my arrival in Punta Arenas, Chile, to my return there
- ***Conditions:*** Temperatures between –20°F (–30°C) and 20°F (–7°C), with weather ranging from calm and clear to blizzards with gusts exceeding 70 mph (115 kph)

IN 1929, BEFORE RICHARD BYRD made his historic flight over the South Pole, he dispatched a hardy team of six dog-mushers led by Dr. Laurence Gould on a 1,500-mile (2,500 km) geological survey across the Ross Ice Shelf into the Trans-Antarctic Mountains. In addition to collecting rock samples from places where no one had traveled before, they were also to act as an emergency rescue squad should Byrd's airplane crash. In honor of the team's efforts, Byrd named prominent mountains after each of its members.

One member was Norman Vaughan, a strapping young Harvard student who would go on to spend much of the rest of his life mushing dogs for search and rescue, for racing, and even for the military during World War II. Due in part to a passion for adventure, he never held a real job for very long, and at age 68 he moved from New England to Alaska, arriving penniless after his third divorce. Nevertheless, his thirst for new challenges endured and after finding work as a janitor, he eked out sufficient money and sponsorship to enable him to repeatedly participate in the state's famed Iditarod—in which

OPPOSITE: Norman Vaughan reacts to his first glimpse of Mount Vaughan. It has been sixty-five years since he first visited the region by dog sled.

he ultimately dubbed himself the "oldest and slowest" participant. (His final run was at age 81; he never officially finished last.)

All the while, however, his dream was to make the first ascent of Mount Vaughan—a financial and logistical impossibility for most of his life. But, by the late 1980s, Giles Kershaw's Adventure Network had established sufficient reach on the continent that Vaughan pondered his own expedition.

Norman's motto was "Dream big and dare to fail." He was willing to risk his life for the summit. Furthermore, he wanted to beat a change in the International Antarctic Treaty, which was going to ban canines on the continent after April 1994. One of the first Americans to mush in Antarctica, he also wanted to be the last. His plan was to fly the dogs to ANI's inland base below the Patriot Hills at 80° S, then mush the remaining 700 miles (1,170 km) to Mount Vaughan, where his team would establish a base camp and climb the mountain.

After two years of fund-raising, Norman's dream nearly reached fruition in 1993. Unfortunately, he made one grave mistake. To save money, he chartered a plane owned by one of ANI's former pilots, who did not share their established ground support. On the morning after Thanksgiving—after taking off with all the expedition's dogs, some of its equipment, and two members (not including Norman and Carolyn, Norman's fourth wife)—the pilot ignored increasingly bad weather reports, flew into a whiteout, and crashed a few miles shy of the bare-ice landing strip at Patriot Hills. Although no one was killed, the team's veterinarian was seriously injured, four dogs fled to their deaths, and Norman's dream appeared shattered.

But Norman did not give up easily. He vowed to mount an expedition the next year—using two Twin

Norman Vaughan reacts to his first glimpse of Mount Vaughan. It has been sixty-five years since he first visited the region by dog sled.

Otters from Patriot Hills rather than a dog team. Because of the planes, Anne Kershaw, who ran ANI after her husband's tragic death in 1990, wanted one of Adventure Network's own guides to lead the expedition. I had worked with the company for several seasons and had traveled to nearly as many locations as some of the pilots, so Anne chose me. Little did I guess that this expedition would prove to involve far more challenges than just getting an 88-year-old man up a 10,300-foot (3,140 m) mountain set less than 300 miles (500 km) from the South Pole.

THE FIRST PEEK

December 3, 1994 (Day 9)

Part of Norman's fund-raising success arose from a rare combination of dogged perseverance and an electric personality enlivened by sparkling eyes and a booming voice. He's a dead ringer for Santa Claus (albeit Santa after a diet). Norman almost always makes people feel happy, and my own mood has been up for the last week, since I first met him in Punta Arenas, Chile.

Norman Vaughan chats with sponsors via satellite phone at Patriot Hills base. This technology did not work at Mount Vaughan; the mountain is so far south the satellite is under the horizon.

OPPOSITE: In accordance with the Antarctic Treaty, Adventure Network removes everything they import to the continent.

I am also cheerful because almost everything is going according to plan. We have landed at Patriot Hills in a C-130 Hercules, practiced climbing techniques (Norman has never before climbed a mountain), and are now stuffed into tiny seats next to a huge pile of equipment aboard a ski-equipped Twin Otter en route to Mount Vaughan. We stop once to refuel, then land again when our pilot, Randy, sees ground fog of unknown expanse. In Antarctica, these low clouds, practically invisible above the white snowscape, can mean death: If you can't see the ground, you cannot land!

Finally, after one of the coldest nights of my life, barely 200 miles (335 km) from the South Pole, we're back in the air and are flying over the Queen Maud Range of the Trans-Antarctic Mountains. Norman and his colleagues mushed here more than sixty-five years ago, and he begins to see landmarks he recog-

Norman Vaughan learns crevasse-rescue techniques before facing the real thing. Acting as if Vern Tejas (upper left) was weighting the rope from a chasm, Norman has collapsed into self-arrest position and is pounding in a snow picket for an anchor.

nizes. Meanwhile, Vern and I gape at granite towers that would beckon any mountaineer. Few have ever been climbed.

Then, Randy leans back out of the cockpit. "Ever seen Mount Vaughan before?" he yells to Norman, who shakes his head. "Well, we're about to fly a few circles around it."

I have never seen a kid beneath a Christmas tree who looked more excited than Norman at that moment. His expression is so entrancing, his exuberant face wrapped in a 4-inch-thick (10 cm) polar-bear-skin lined hood, that I completely forget to take any slides of his mountain and focus only on him.

Landing conditions are perfect. After circling low above the ground to visually check for crevasses, our Twin Otter's skis plow into a foot (0.3 m) of new snow atop a tributary of the Amundsen Glacier. We taxi to what appears to be a good campsite, the film crew jumps out, and I bolt after them. Each of us captures Norman stepping onto the snow in front of his mountain. Within minutes he and Carolyn are in tears, and they pull the hat off Vern's shaved head to give it a kiss.

BIRTHDAY BATTLE

December 8, 1994 (Day 14)

The last few days have been busy. We have established a virtually weatherproof base camp with huge, snow-block walls protecting every tent, and Vern dug a clever sunken dining area. A second plane has arrived carrying more supplies and crew, including Alejo, Rob Hart, my old friend and assistant leader, and two other climbers who will carry loads and help to pay for the trip. Vern and I have even led Norman and Carolyn on a practice mission halfway to Camp One, which Norman plans to name Camp Goodale, after one of his companions on his 1929 sledging journey. All of our camps will be similarly named, beginning with base camp, dubbed Camp deGanahl.

Norman is feeling good today and it is time to start moving up the mountain. Vern and I have scurried most of the way to the top to investigate conditions. The round-trip took us less than four hours. We guess, however, that Norman will need a week to nine days, assuming modestly good weather and no attempt to delay a summit bid until Norman's 89th birthday—December 19—eleven days away.

Even before I left the States, Anne Kershaw told me that Norman's birthday had been a touchy issue. Norman, Carolyn, and Vern wanted to wait for the big day. The film crew, pilots, and Anne all want him to reach the summit at the first possible opportunity, knowing that he may get only one chance. Anne was so concerned that she made Norman sign a contract stating that his birthday was to have absolutely no weight when making decisions, and to my dismay, as a representative of Adventure Network I have to enforce this. I know how easily a little stall here and a bad day there can add up to just enough extra time to make that birthday ascent a reality. Yet, those stalls could as easily delay us into a storm and failure.

We begin climbing at 11:15 A.M. and maintain a good pace, measured both by Norman's electronic heart monitor and periodic stops that allow Vern to manually take Norman's pulse. Not once does it rise above 110 beats a minute—a rate many couch potatoes exceed when watching a horror movie. Norman's biggest problem is his plastic knee and fused ankle, which make the cocked foot positions necessary for steep snow climbing very difficult. The most difficult section of the climb is a knife-edged ridge that is

FOLLOWING SPREAD: The exploratory team on the southwest ridge of Mount Vaughan.

OPPOSITE: Expedition members set up Camp Goodale, which, due to Norman's slow pace, is almost within shouting distance of Camp deGanahl (base camp).

Guide Vern Tejas shaves his head as Norman Vaughan enjoys his breakfast cereal at Camp deGanahl.

Norman Vaughan starts up the southwest ridge of Mount Vaughan, carrying Zippy, a stuffed dog that represents canine contributions to Antarctic exploration. After being one of the first Americans to mush on the continent in 1929, he had hoped to be the last.

inclined nearly 30°; there is no chance of deviating to either side. Norman will have to "duck walk" his way up. I climb most of the way facing backward, four feet (1.3 m) above him, and he makes it to the camp in relatively good time. Perhaps we stand a chance.

COLD WINDS AND HOT AIR

December 11, 1994 (Day 17)

We have suffered from miserable weather for the last two days—bad enough to keep Norman stuck in his tent, but not so ferocious that Rob, Barry, and some of the flight crew couldn't carry more food and fuel up to Camp Goodale. All team members except for Norman and Carolyn climbed to Camp II, dubbed Camp Crockett, to hack out preliminary tent platforms.

Yesterday was particularly bad. Although we woke at two in the morning to blue sky, the weather quickly deteriorated. Norman was relieved to stay put, but soon gusts exceeding 60 mph (100 kph) began toppling the snow walls protecting our tents. One nearly crushed Norman's head and another Larry's camera gear, and we were up for hours rebuilding our defenses.

This morning, however, the sun shone fitfully, the wind had diminished, and we debated what to do. Radio messages from Patriot Hills urged us to make

Vern Tejas leads Norman Vaughan and Carolyn Muegge-Vaughan up to Camp Crockett.

haste. Our planes were needed elsewhere. Barry and Bob (who call themselves Team M & M, money and muscle) are worried that our slow progress means they will miss not only Christmas with their families but also vital year-end financial juggling to limit their taxes. To keep up momentum, Alejo, Vern, the film crew, and I all carry loads to Camp Crockett and set up tents.

When we descend back to Camp Goodale, Rob, Barry, and Bob have arrived with additional gear and agree to carry it onward, although Bob says, "If this expedition doesn't get moving faster, I won't get mad, I'll get even." I wonder how.

Norman and Carolyn agree to move up, despite frigid temperatures and on-again, off-again blizzards. Both are very slow, but we reach Camp Crockett in three hours. Norman suffers a touch of snow blindness en route, and after collapsing into his tent has to keep cold cloths over his eyes.

SIMMERING TENSIONS

December 15, 1994 (Day 21)

By now dissension is brewing. Bob and Barry are upset that Carolyn wants this to be solely Norman's expedition and will not allow them to camp with the rest of us on the mountain. They feel they have been misled and have been relegated to second class status. As a consequence, they simply want to go home. This morning they even radioed Punta Arenas to demand that one of our Twin Otters fly them out; their request was refused. Realizing the only way out is up, they want Norman to reach the top as

soon as possible and are second-guessing every radio transmission about our progress (or lack thereof).

In an attempt to ameliorate the situation, I asked Rob Hart to guide Bob and Barry for whatever else they might want to do. Rob wants to climb other mountains, but is frustrated, stuck in camp while his clients sulk. I can't believe that they're not climbing and skiing everything in sight. On either side of Mount Vaughan march a legion of virgin, very accessible summits. Even if they can't climb side-by-side with Norman, how many other times will they ever get an opportunity such as this?

Meanwhile, Vern and I have again climbed to within a few steps of the summit, scoping out the route. We realize that Norman does not have the stamina to reach it from Camp Crockett, a distance of 1,000 vertical feet (300 m). We still need Camp III. We establish Camp Gould in the shadow of a wind-breaking serac, the last shelter before the top, and this afternoon we move both Norman and Carolyn into it. Vern stays with them and I descend back to Camp Crockett for the night.

ON TOP OF THE WORLD

December 16 & 17, 1994 (Days 22 & 23)

Today the weather is perfect and I hear via private, unscheduled radio transmissions and tent-to-tent chatter that everyone in base camp, as well as the film crew and Alejo, who are camped beside me, believe that the summit is nigh. But when I radio up to Camp Gould (which everyone can overhear) Carolyn reports, "Norman is tired." I sign off and instantly hear unprintable swearing from the adjacent tent. Even I, who have a personality resembling a golden retriever, am upset.

Vern Tejas cooks at Camp Crockett.

"Yeah," said someone best left nameless. "He'll moan and groan until the nineteenth, then suddenly he'll be charging like a stallion!"

Today is the day for which I was hired to be an asshole to someone, and I try to base my decision on the facts. I know that Norman really is tired. Another day or two of rest would do him good and increase his chances. And by then, why not just wait another day for his birthday?

Counterbalancing this are weather reports from the U.S. science station at McMurdo Bay, which suggest we are at the end of a high-pressure cycle and could be in for some serious weather of unknown duration. I think back on some of the week-long—even two-week-long—storms I have endured and realize that if one of those hits, Norman won't only fail to reach the summit on his birthday, he won't reach it at all. He might even be killed.

I conclude there is no choice and I head back up to Camp Gould, where I chance upon Norman's tent at a lucky moment; both Carolyn and Vern are occupied with morning constitutionals.

"Norman," I say, "I know that you want to climb Mount Vaughan on your birthday. But Antarctica is Antarctica. You know as well as I do that you act when the weather is good. Today is the day." Overcoming his obvious exhaustion, he agrees without argument and begins packing. When Carolyn gets back to the tent she grudgingly agrees, but when Vern returns, he is furious.

"Are you going to risk Norman's life just to fit Adventure Network's flight schedules?" he demands. Although Vern and I have become very close on this expedition, I don't understand his willingness to delay. He knows enough about polar weather to recognize that we have no business sitting around as it starts to deteriorate. I wonder if Norman, Carolyn and Vern are mistakenly overemphasizing the

Norman Vaughan catches his breath en route to the summit. (Carolyn Muegge-Vaughan is in the background.)

Carolyn Muegge-Vaughan attempts to light 89 sparklers atop Norman's "cake" to celebrate his upcoming birthday.

public relations potential of reaching the summit on his birthday and are therefore stalling. Wasn't the summit enough? By now Alejo and the film crew have also arrived at Camp Gould, and they agree with me. The birthday would be icing, Larry and Peter acknowledge, but without a summit, they have no film at all.

Ultimately Vern acquiesces, but only after stating that Norman's death (from exhaustion) will be on our hands. We set forth on what will prove to be a brutal day. Sometimes I think that Norman will collapse, but under Carolyn's loving care and constant infusion of nutrients, he keeps going. Within a few hours we pass the steepest section and are nearly upon the summit. Larry, Peter, and I rush ahead, stopping a few meters shy of the summit to film Norman striding boldly to the top, becoming the first man to climb the mountain. As each of us keep our cameras rolling, he hugs Carolyn, then rips off Vern's hat to kiss his shaved head once again. Norman reads a tribute to his 1929 partners and their dogs, and Carolyn futilely tries to light eighty-nine sparklers atop Mount Vaughan—

Norman Vaughan, exhausted in his tent at Camp deGanahl after descent from summit.

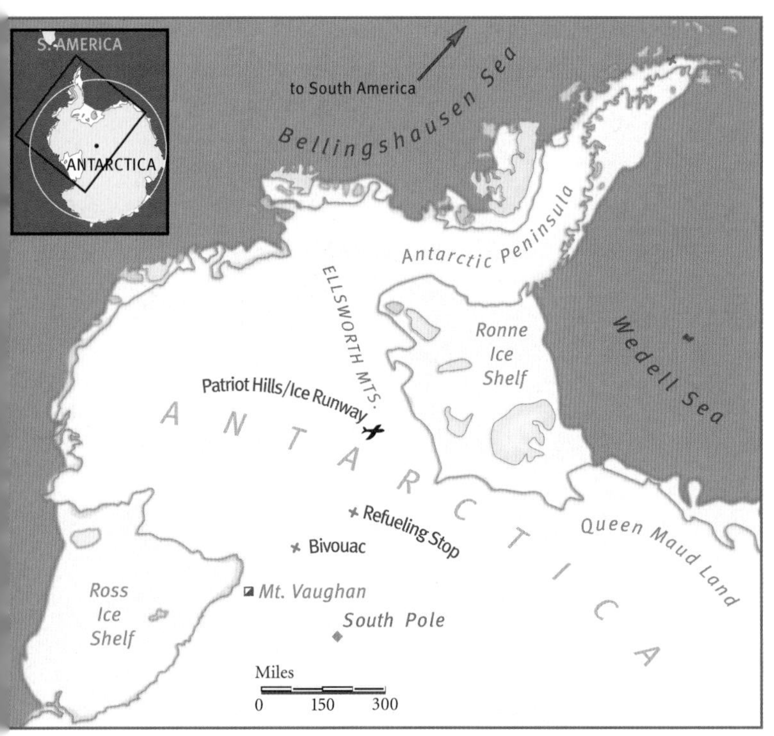

his birthday cake—to celebrate. The wind blows all of them out.

Moments later, Norman nearly faints. We pitch a tent on the summit and spend a frightening night wondering whether he will perish from hypothermia. After many cups of tea and hot soup, however, he revives and with the help of a sled and a rope, we finally lower him back to the bottom.

As our airplane revs its engines to depart from base camp, he promises, "I'm going to return to celebrate my one-hundredth birthday."*

* Norman did attempt to do this, but could not procure the funding. He died peacefully, four days after celebrating the event with scores of friends at a hospital in Anchorage.

OPPOSITE: Norman Vaughan and Carolyn Muegge-Vaughan enjoy a last view of Mount Vaughan before the Twin Otter returns them to Patriot Hills base.

CHAPTER FIVE

CHASING THE INDOMITABLE WILL

Across the Arctic Ocean, 1995

- ***Location:*** A 1,100-mile (1,800 km) route from Cape Arkticheskiy, on Russia's Severnaya Zemlya archipelago (81° N, 96° E) to Canada's Ward Hunt Island (83° N, 79° W) via the North Pole
- ***Team:*** Will Steger (leader), Dr. Victor Boyarsky, Takano Takako (who is called by her given name, Takako), Julie Hanson, Martin Hignell, Ulrik Vedel, and Paul Pregont
- ***Dates:*** March 8 to July 3, 1995
- ***Conditions:*** A wide mix, ranging from clear and cold, with temperatures lower than −45°F (−43°C), to blizzards, to sunny, twenty-four-hour days with temperatures enough above freezing to create slushy snow and a diminishing ice pack

BY 1991, EXPLORER WILL STEGER HAD PUSHED THE LIMITS of human and canine endurance in both the Arctic and Antarctica. In 1986 he co-led the first confirmed, unsupported dog sled expedition to the North Pole, and three years later he mushed 3,741 miles (6,021 km) across Antarctica—from the tip of the Antarctic Peninsula to the South Pole, and onward to a Soviet science base at Mirny. These are hard acts to follow, but Will is not a man to bask in his achievements.

Will Steger, shortly after departing Cape Arkticheskiy at the beginning of the International Arctic Project Expedition across the Arctic Ocean.

Will is passionate about earth's global environment, which he believes to be imperiled. He also cares deeply about educating people—especially schoolchildren—about the many relationships between the natural wonders he encounters on his journeys and planetary ecological change. To him, this seemed like the perfect inspiration for another polar undertaking.

OPPOSITE: Will Steger's dogs race across relatively flat sea ice, a rare occurrence.

Victor Boyarsky logs progress of the 1989–90 Trans-Antarctica Expedition on the wall of his tent at South Pole.

Shortly after his Trans-Antarctica Expedition, Will began planning another dog sled journey across the opposite end of the planet. His goal was to traverse the formidable, frozen Arctic Ocean using only dogs and human muscle, and also to use new satellite and Internet technology to communicate daily with thousands of students around the world. In addition to describing their adventures and the endlessly entertaining antics of the dogs, he and the team would also relay a coordinated lesson plan on Arctic and global ecology.

Because Will had become famous for living up to his sponsors' expectations, he quickly secured funding from three companies—Lands' End, Shaklee, and 3M—all of which manufacture products the team could use and test. *National Geographic*'s editor, William Graves, confidently bought the first rights to Will's story and pictures, despite objections from some colleagues, who thought that the magazine had covered enough polar dog sledding.

Takano Takako fights to avoid toppling into an open water lead after Martin Hignell's sled broke through thin ice during a 1994 training mission on the Arctic Ocean. I had already fallen through to my waist, and Martin blamed my presence next to the lead (in expectation of a picture) for luring his dogs into the water.

To give this undertaking the broadest appeal, Will chose his team members from five different countries, and called his endeavor the International Arctic Project. First to join him was Dr. Victor Boyarsky, a Russian physicist who had crossed Antarctica with Will. Then, over the course of three extended training expeditions to northern Canada, he invited Ulrik Vedel, who had spent several seasons sledging the east coast of Greenland with Denmark's famed Sirius Patrol; Martin Hignell, a veteran dog trainer and handler with three seasons' Antarctic experience at Britain's Rothera science base; Julie Hanson, a biology teacher and outdoor education instructor who lived in Will's home town of Ely, Minnesota; and Takano Takako, a writer for the *Japan Times* and leader of various Japanese wilderness programs.

I first joined the team for a week during the second training exercise. Will's sponsors needed a photographer to show their products in use, and I had already photographed his Trans-Antarctica Expedition at the South Pole. Will and I had become friends, so he suggested me for the job. I returned for another ten days the following year. Finally, I was selected by *National Geographic* to accompany the team during key periods at the beginning, middle, and end of the actual journey across the ocean.

Chicago, an aggressive sled dog, growls at another canine in the team.

AN ICY SWIM

March 9, 1995 (Day 2)

We have reached the launching point of our expedition, a lonely beach called Cape Arkticheskiy, after flying from Golomianiy Weather Station the day before. Outside my tent the temperature is somewhere below –45°F (–43°C). Last night Will's toothpaste and his Scotch froze solid. Wind rattles the tent's fly, and I wonder if I will survive until the helicopter that is scheduled to retrieve me arrives around noon (the team does not want me to accompany them very far during this unpredictable first stage). I also wonder if the team members are out of their minds to leave the land in such hostile conditions.

I step outside shortly after sunrise to shoot camp scenes in rich, golden light. As usual, I quickly reach the end of a roll and remove my gloves to change it. At least my trusty, all mechanical Nikon FM2, which I have winterized with special lubricants, is still working. Most electronic cameras would have failed. After only thirty seconds exposed to the air, however, both of my hands are as white as the snow around me. I can scarcely feel them as I slam the camera closed. I dive for the tent and thaw them over a stove. Three minutes later, the color returns to my fingers.

Promptly at 8:30, Will yells for everyone to tear down the tents and pack their kamatiks, simple but sturdy wood sledges that are lashed together in a design that can twist and bend through contorted ice. I am astonished by how quickly they load each of these with 1,300 pounds (590 kg) of equipment, provisions, and dog food—top-heavy piles almost 4 feet (1.3 m) high. Will wonders whether the animals can even drag them. No sooner are all the beasts harnessed, however, than their pent-up energy from days of inactivity bursts into forward motion. We have to run on our skis to keep up. I try to snap pictures without breaking stride, and every film change threatens to leave me hopelessly behind.

The light is beautiful and the frozen seascape

LEFT: Ulrik Vedel performs life-saving mouth-to-mouth resuscitation on Diesel after the dog nearly strangled in its traces while jumping a lead during the 1994 training mission.

Julie Hanson checks her sled at the expedition's camp on Cape Arkticheskiy. Temperatures on this night before departure onto the Arctic Ocean were about −45°F (−43°C)—cold enough to freeze Will Steger's celebratory Scotch.

magnificent, but danger lurks everywhere. Will's sled suddenly catches on a big block of ice that had been squeezed up in a pressure ridge and tips over onto him, nearly breaking his leg. Then, just as he, Julie, and I get it righted, we hear shouts from ahead.

I scoot forward around huge ice blocks and see Ulrik pulling himself out of the ocean. He starts madly jumping up and down, whirling his arms to generate circulation in his numb fingers. His clothes are freezing solid. Not far away, across a now-open lead, a long, open-water crack in the ice, Victor is also crawling from the sea.

I quickly hand Ulrik my extra gloves; Julie sets up a tent and lights a stove. His story emerges. After an hour and a half of relatively smooth sailing, Victor, who was skiing ahead to lead the way, encountered a sudden maze of pressure ridges separated by barely frozen bands of slush. While he was circling around one, Ulrik's lead dog bolted straight for him and broke through, dragging the others with him. Because they were all still harnessed, the team started to sink and both Ulrik and Victor jumped in to cut them loose. If they hadn't, Ulrik's dogs would have drowned and his sled sunk hundreds of feet to the ocean bottom. What had been a typically miserable morning is now an emergency.

Ulrik Vedel's dog team races onto the Arctic Ocean from Cape Arkticheskiy at the onset of the expedition.

BELOW: Ulrik Vedel and Victor Boyarsky in −40°F (−40°C) after jumping into the ocean to save drowning dogs.

HELL FROZEN OVER

March 12, 1995 (Day 5)

This afternoon, I tag along as our helicopter (the same one that whisked me off the ice just after Ulrik and Victor fell through) flies back out to rejoin the expedition for an aerial reconnaissance. By the time we reach the team, it has retreated back to a camp on shore and everyone looks shell-shocked. Ulrik seems especially rattled. As we load most of the group aboard and fly out over the most tortured looking ice any of them has ever seen, he relates what happened since he fell into the sea.

The last three days, he says, have been "hell frozen over." No sooner did he and Victor re-warm themselves in an emergency campsite than Will fell sick and a snowstorm kicked up. Then as much as 30 miles (40 km) of water suddenly yawned open ahead of them.

Under the best of conditions, the team's location was perilous. Thousands of square miles of floating ice, propelled several miles a day by winds and ocean currents, crush into the shores of Cape Arkticheskiy; an irresistible force meeting an immovable object. The result is chaos. After a single night at their first offshore campsite, the team decided to retreat to shore and regroup. Unfortunately, the ice was then so tortured that retreating the distance that required just two hours on the outbound journey took two days.

Nowhere does the ice appear to be solid, and pans that seem safe suddenly either split in half and start moving apart, or crush together and pile into massive pressure ridges; ice blocks the size of automobiles tumble and roll forward as if pushed by some Herculean bulldozer. Sometimes one sled traverses a short distance, and then a lead opens and pre-

vents the others from following. Meanwhile, turning a 40-foot-long (12 m) dog team around can take half an hour or longer, while a cacophony of frightening noises crashes and rumbles. Worse, they have already seen several polar bears, which are just emerging from their dens, hungry, and can attack at any moment.

I watch Ulrik's expression turn to horror as we chopper over hundreds of square miles of tortured sea ice. "There's no way we're going to survive out there," he tells me.

A Russian meteorologist at Golomianiy braces against sub-zero winds at the weather station on Severnaya Zemlya archipelago, the last "civilization" the team would encounter for 118 days.

THE EMPTY QUARTER

April 3, 1995 (Day 27)

Ulrik quit the expedition on March 13, taking with him all of his dogs. The rest of the group rearranges their loads and all logistics. For more than two weeks they camp at Cape Arkticheskiy—a place they call Desperation Camp—until finally a Russian helicopter picks them up and ferries them 300 miles (480 km) north, past the worst of the tortured ice. They now have nineteen days to reach the North Pole—a distance of about 250 miles (350 km)—in order to reach it in time for Earth Day, April 22. During that period, there will be little hope of any rescue or resupply.

INTO THE DRINK AGAIN

April 27, 1995 (Day 51)

Shortly after I fly in to the North Pole on the first of two planes carrying heavy loads of food and equipment, a few key sponsors, and a film crew from ABC's *Good Morning America,* the entourage departs. This morning is beautiful, we load the sleds quickly, and I team up with Will as we start sledging south, a bearing that is somewhat meaningless, because *any* direction is south. Unfortunately, because we have drifted more than 25 miles (40 km) in the wrong direction over the last five days, complicating navigation. In terms of longitude, we are now almost a quarter of the way around the world from our intended course. Will fears that it will take us many days—even weeks—to get back to the line he wants to follow to Canada.

Nevertheless, we're laughing about the wonderful, 0°F (–18°C) weather when I hear a commotion ahead. "Get up there!" shouts Will. "There might be a picture!"

He's right. While Victor was navigating around a patch of deceptively thin ice, Martin's dog disobeyed his "whoa" command, bolted, and the back of Martin's sled broke through. At least the dogs remained dry and several have climbed back onto thicker ice. Although the scene looks innocent enough—something like a truck stuck in a frozen creek—it is perilous. Here the Arctic Ocean is more than two miles deep, and if the front of the sled breaks through, it will instantly sink and drag every animal in after it. Both

OPPOSITE: After sharing transportation to Severnaya Zemlya with Will Steger, Reinhold and Hubert Messner ski on the frozen Arctic Ocean. Sadly, their attempt to man-haul sledges from Russia to Canada via the North Pole was quickly thwarted by the same dangerous ice conditions that plagued Will's expedition. After two days, they had to be rescued.

Victor and Martin join the dogs to pull with all of their might, and Will quickly dashes up to pitch in. I try to lend a hand, but Will orders me to stop.

"Take pictures!" he yells.

PERPETUAL MOTION

May 10, 1995 (Day 64)

Every day brings new challenges and thrilling moments, but for me, after traveling only two weeks south of the pole, they are already blending together, relentlessly ruled by Will's strict routines. Perhaps that's the only way to keep going across an expanse as big as this one. Every morning we wake at 6:30, light our stoves, and cook breakfast. Everyone heads out for a bathroom break, and no matter what the temperature, Victor emerges naked to bathe in the snow.

Precisely at 8:15, triggered by some mysterious body clock, every dog starts howling for a minute, then falls silent, waiting for us to unzip our tent doors at exactly 8:30, disassemble our shelters, load the sleds, and harness them up. By 9:00, if not earlier, they are leaping at their traces and barking to go. Except for unpredictable stops when we have to chop our way through pressure ice—which sometimes seems to stretch for miles—we move relentlessly until 12:00 sharp, when we stop for lunch. At 12:15 the dogs howl again, and by 12:30 we're back underway until 5:00, when we search for a campsite. After pitching tents and tossing camping gear inside, one person from each team lights the stove to melt water while the other stakes out the dogs and feeds them. Afterward dinner is generally leisurely, followed by a satellite transmission to the Internet (my first day at the pole, we also sent a digital photo—the first ever beamed from there). Finally, when all work is done, there are a few moments to read or write before sleep. Then, except for rare rest days, the routine repeats itself exactly the following morn. The sun never sets.

Will Steger and Victor Boyarsky struggle to help the dogs pull Martin Hignell's sled out of a lead near the North Pole, where the Arctic Ocean is over 10,000 feet (3,000 m) deep.

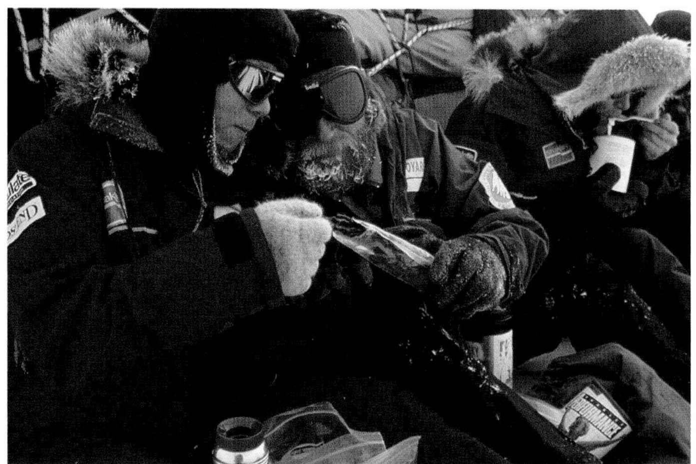

CLOCKWISE FROM TOP LEFT: Takano Takako and Victor Boyarsky share dried venison during a lunch stop in the lee of a sled.

Takano Takako and Julie Hanson steer their sled between leads and pressure ridges as they work southward from the pole.

The dogs enjoy their daily noon howl.

A sled dog wakes under insulating snow after spending a windy "night" on the frozen Arctic Ocean.

Victor Boyarsky begins his morning with a snow bath, regardless of the weather.

Takano Takako and Julie Hanson delight as they compose a daily message for schoolchildren to be uploaded via satellite to the Internet.

Will Steger's team crosses a pressure ridge.

RIGHT: This lead cracked through the middle of a camp that had appeared to be situated on solid ice. In minutes the fissure widened to 30 feet (10 m), nearly drowning some of Martin Hignell's dogs, which were staked to a line anchored on each side.

FOLLOWING SPREAD: Expedition members drag canoe-sleds toward the end of their journey at Canada's Ward Hunt Island.

PRESSURE ICE

May 15, 1995 (Day 69)

Before I flew in to join the team at the pole, Will assured me that I'd only be with them for about ten days before a plane would come to drop off supplies and take me out. But when I arrived on April 22, he had learned that expedition funds were growing thin and he couldn't afford the flight. Instead, he told me, I'd be with them for at least three weeks. Today it is plain that my departure is still several days away. All told, in the course of his 1,100-mile (1,800 km) journey, there will be only three resupply flights: one at the pole, one to pick me up, and a last one to pick up the dogs and replace them with the canoes that Will hopes will get the team to land.

Yet I have fallen into the swing of things. Crossing the Arctic Ocean is more scenic, interesting, and challenging than slogging across its counterpart, the Antarctic ice cap. Because of pressure ice, the scenery seldom seems vast and harbors a certain ever-changing intimacy. Even if there is scarcely another soul in any direction, I don't feel like I'm in the middle of nowhere.

Nevertheless, danger is always but a misstep away. Today I take off my skis to help chop at ice blocking the sleds and nearly fall through new snow into the ocean. Then we get almost hopelessly separated from Martin. Shortly after reaching a narrow ice bridge separating two large areas of open water, Martin coaxes his team across. Before Takako and Julie can follow, however, currents tear the bridge in half. As we watch, Martin's side drifts away as quickly as a train leaving its platform. "See you at Christmas!" he jokes halfheartedly. Although each sled team is self-sufficient with food, fuel and shelter for exactly this contingency, being separated could still be deadly. It takes us four hours of meticulous route-finding and detours to rejoin him.

DRAGGING BACK TO LAND

July 3, 1995 (Day 118)

Four days earlier, I flew north from a jet airstrip at Resolute Bay on Arctic Canada's Cornwallis Island in hope of rejoining the team before they came ashore at Ward Hunt Island, one of the northernmost points in Canada. Unfortunately, mechanics had traded the bush plane's skis for tundra tires, and although we spotted the team from the air, the snow was much too soft for a landing.

OPPOSITE: Takano Takako leads Will Steger's dogs over an open water lead.

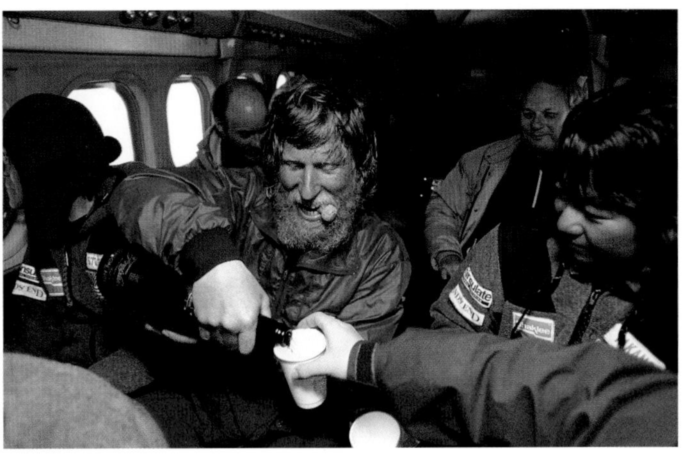

Victor Boyarsky pours celebratory champagne aboard the Twin Otter en route to Resolute Bay and civilization.

Now, after spending the last few days at a remote weather station on Ellesmere Island, killing time photographing arctic wolves and hares, I've joined a Canadian customs official and several of the team's friends and family members to fly back to Ward Hunt. We land just in time for the expedition's arrival on shore. As Victor lights flares and the team pours mugs of champagne we had brought, I hear a few tales and am instantly grateful that my earlier flight had been unable to land.

Almost a month after I last saw the team on May 18, another resupply flight had picked up all of the dogs and left canoes specially designed with sled runners on the bottom. Also on the plane was Paul Pregont, a new, sixth expedition member, who had been recruited at the last minute to help with what would prove to be the journey's most brutal stage.

By that point, the snow was so rotten and leads so frequent that there was no hope of using the dogs to get to shore. Will had anticipated this from the very start, and the canoes were to be their salvation. They were not, however, an easy one. Instead of sliding smoothly, they bogged into deep, new-fallen snow. Pulling them often felt like dragging huge bags of cement, and every pressure ridge seemed an insurmountable challenge. Only on rare occasions could they paddle more than a few meters, and then getting the heavily laden boats back onto the ice was an epic struggle. Despite toiling for up to ten hours a day, they sometimes made only a few miles. By the time the team finally reached Ward Hunt, they were brutalized.

As we greet them, however, they are also exuberant about accomplishing a feat few could endure. In a flourish of victory, Julie spots some saxifrage and pulls it up to her nose. She had all but forgotten the smell of land.

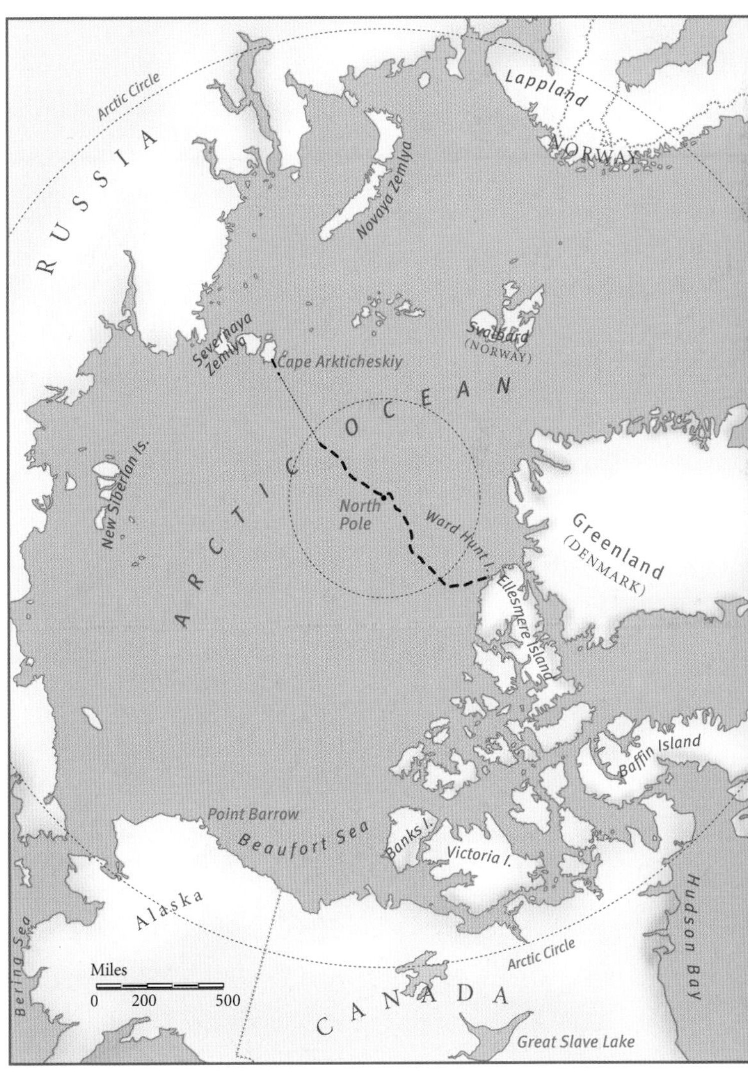

CHAPTER SIX

SCALING THE RAZOR

Rakekniven, Queen Maud Land, Antarctica, 1997

- ***Location:*** Rakekniven, Queen Maud Land, Antarctica; 71° S; 7° E; about 2,700 miles (4,500 km) south of Cape Town, South Africa, and 120 miles (200 km) southeast of India's Maitri science base in the portion of Antarctica claimed by Norway
- ***Team:*** Gordon Wiltsie (organizational leader), Alex Lowe, Conrad Anker, Rick Ridgeway, Michael Graber, and Jon Krakauer
- ***Dates:*** December 1, 1996, to January 17, 1997, from my arrival in Cape Town until our return
- ***Conditions:*** Twenty-four-hour daylight with temperatures ranging between −10°F (−18°C) to 10°F (−12°C), depending on wind chill and shadows. Mysteriously, we were in a "wind shadow"; this climb was protected from nearby gusts that exceeded 100 mph (165 kph).

BY 1996, ALEX LOWE HAD CLIMBED IN SO MANY PLACES around the world, and with such astonishing speed, grace, and style, that even legendary mountaineer Reinhold Messner called him the greatest living alpinist. He was so far beyond my own humble abilities—and both of us were on the road so often—that even though our children played together in my adopted home town of Bozeman, we didn't meet in person until he was invited to join a sailboat-based climbing expedition to the Antarctic Peninsula.

He knew that I had traveled widely there and wanted my advice. We quickly recognized each other as kindred spirits and our conversation stretched to a lonely place called Queen Maud Land, which I soon would be visiting on a "secret" aerial reconnaissance for Adventure Network. Two years earlier, a Norwegian group led by Ivar Tollefsen had traveled there on a freighter that resupplied Russian science bases, and in just the month that the ship was unloading the Norwegians had climbed numerous mountains of unearthly beauty. Shortly before my conversation with Alex, Ivar had published a book, and I told Alex about the region's astonishing potential.

ABOVE: This picture of Rakekniven, shot from the north, was the image that first inspired Alex Lowe to climb in Queen Maud Land.

OPPOSITE: Conrad Anker jumars high above the polar ice cap.

FOLLOWING SPREAD: Jon Krakauer and Conrad Anker cross-country ski near Rakekniven. Our expedition climbed the right-hand skyline.

Six weeks later, on the scouting mission, I learned that Queen Maud Land was even more spectacular (and dangerous) than I first envisioned. Bad weather pinned us down several times—including one storm so fierce that it nearly blew away our plane. What was supposed to be a one-week trip stretched to three. Nevertheless, I was awestruck by the mountains in front of my lenses. Huge, vertical granite fangs chomped through ice a mile (2 km) thick. One, called Rakekniven (The Razor), especially impressed me. This summit, in the Filchner Mountains, was shaped exactly like a shark's fin, with a blank, eastern wall that overhung for more than 2,000 feet (600 m)—taller than the fabled west face of Yosemite's Half Dome.

As I expected, Alex was ecstatic when I showed him pictures. So, too, was his long-time climbing partner, Conrad Anker, who was himself famous for pioneering bold new lines up cliffs like Yosemite's El Capitan, and for being one of the few high-altitude climbers who could keep Alex in sight. Together, we met with Bill Simon, CEO of The North Face, Conrad and Alex's sponsor, and he assured us that if I could sell an expedition to *National Geographic,* he would underwrite a proportionate share of our funding.

Meanwhile, Peter Miller, the expeditions editor at *National Geographic,* was equally intrigued. So was Rick Ridgeway, a famed adventure author, filmmaker, and mountaineer who had seen Tollefsen's book and was cajoling Peter to be the official writer for any team the magazine might assign to go there. To Rick's dismay, however, the magazine's editorial board accepted my proposal, but wanted Jon Krakauer—a best-selling author who had just survived a debacle on Mount Everest—to pen the account. If Rick wanted to join us, he would have to raise his own sponsorship, most likely from television. In the interim, the rest of us began planning without him.

For Rick, the ensuing six months dealt one rejection after another. By mid-November—two weeks before our departure—he had still not secured any funding. Even though Conrad, Alex, and I all wanted both him and his proposed cameraman, Michael Graber (a veteran mountaineer and one of my oldest friends), to join us, we agreed that it was too late to add them to the team. Rick called the very next morning. Based on a totally rewritten proposal, *National Geographic Explorer* finally wanted a film. Even though Mike was in China, knew nothing of this recent development, and had already promised his wife, Diana Schulz, that he'd be home for Christmas, Rick swore that the two of them would be ready to leave with the rest of us.

ONTO THE ICE

December 21, 1996 (Day 21)

More than three weeks after leaving home, we are in base camp. After delays due to political snags and panicked efforts to track down aircraft parts—during which we climbed famous cliffs around Cape Town—Adventure Network's C-130 Hercules finally made its first passenger flight to the bare-ice glacier we found on our scouting mission the season before. Now, after resting and re-sorting our equipment, we have flown another 45 miles (75 km) to Rakekniven in a ski-equipped Twin Otter.

Before unloading, we all run through knee-deep snow to touch the rock we will be climbing. Alex scrambles thirty feet up a thin crack and proclaims, "This is incredible! It's as solid as Yosemite!"

Everyone whoops and hugs as we return to the plane, which pilot Greg Stein taxis straight to a scenic campsite. We offload everything, and as Greg departs, buzzing low overhead, I feel an overwhelming rush of loneliness in a setting so vast that it dwarfs even our loftiest ambitions.

Quickly we assemble our tents, gulp a reconstituted freeze-dried dinner, and revel in our good fortune to be here. Five miles (8 km) south, big snow plumes are boiling off a mountain called Kubus, painted pink in the low-angle light, and I momentarily remember horrifying nearby storms that surprised us during our scouting expedition last year. I pray that one won't similarly trap us on the wall. We linger outside until the sun finally circles behind Rakekniven (it would never actually set while we were there) and temperatures plummet so far, so fast, that we have to dive into our sleeping bags.

OPPOSITE: Adventure Network guide Mike Sharp in a stormy camp during a scouting trip in January 1996.

TOP: Alex Lowe glimpses Rakekniven for the first time.

MIDDLE: The C-130 Hercules getting refueled from cached drums at Blue One, an ice runway in Queen Maud Land.

BOTTOM: The Twin Otter leaves our expedition at Rakekniven base camp.

ABOVE: High winds blow spindrift off Mount Kubus.

BELOW: Michael Graber prepares to film Alex Lowe digging out new-fallen snow at Rakekniven base camp.

PLUMMETING ROCKS

December 23, 1996 (Day 23)

After climbing two pitches yesterday afternoon, Alex is forging up an intimidating crack that demands the use of artificial aid—climbing with pitons and sling ladders—while Conrad belays him from below. Meanwhile, Mike, Rick, and I climb an adjacent ridge where we get long shots straight across at them with our telephotos. Through my 400mm lens I can almost see Alex's facial expressions as he inches toward a huge flake that looks so unstable a single caress might dislodge it, a horrifying prospect that would crush Alex and Conrad into paste. Yesterday Conrad had barely climbed halfway up the first pitch before realizing that Rakekniven was far less stable than Alex first pronounced. Every few feet he encountered loose stones ranging in size from golf balls to cement sacks. Even solid-looking faces were crumbly. All afternoon, the rest of us cowered beneath an overhang as pebbles and boulders whistled down. My own enthusiasm for the climb plummeted nearly as quickly. Nothing has ever come closer to killing me than falling rock.

ABOVE: The expedition team is dwarfed by Rakekniven's east face. The route ascends the prominent crack system splitting the wall.

RIGHT: Conrad Anker belays as Alex Lowe leads the fourth pitch. From my vantage, I worried that the huge flake above Alex would peel loose if he pulled on it.

Gordon Wiltsie jumars into camera position high up Rakekniven. PHOTO BY RICK RIDGEWAY

Fortunately, the flake above Alex is more solid than it appears and he quickly grapples past it. Nevertheless, his overall progress is slow. Mike and I periodically nap between shouts of "Slack!" "How much rope is left?" and "Watch out, I'm hurling off a rock!" By afternoon they complete two more pitches, reaching the only big ledge on the climb, which they dub the Sun Deck.

A WORKING HOLIDAY

December 25, 1996 (Day 25)

Because today is both Christmas and the day after Alex's birthday, Conrad suggested last night that we all rest. Aside from these obvious excuses, Alex's hands are so bloodied from jamming them into cracks that he can scarcely grasp a cup. I relish the chance to sleep guilt-free until noon, but Rick—ever an early bird—

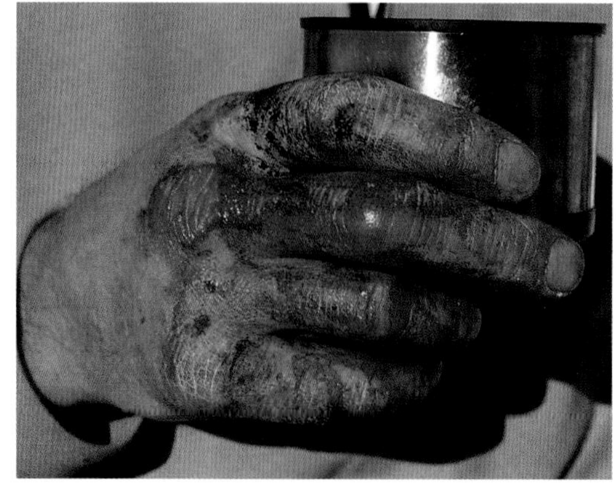

RIGHT: Jon Krakauer takes notes in a base camp tent.

wakes at 4 A.M., heads for the cook tent, and bangs around while brewing a pot of coffee. He settles back into his own tent, right next to the one I share with Alex, rouses Mike, and starts talking. I grouse at them once, but they might as well have set off an alarm clock. By 6 A.M., everyone is up.

I still plan to goof off, but during breakfast Jon suggests that I haul a load up to the Sun Deck to get more comfortable on the wall. My initial reaction is dread. Two days earlier, a stone smashed Rick on the nose. Much bigger ones litter the snow. I know that every second I spend on the climb reduces my survival odds and dying on Christmas would be one hell of a present for my family.

Still, there is no honorable escape. Together with Rick, Jon, and Mike, I ski half an hour to the bottom of our ropes and ratchet upward. Yesterday, just the first 200 feet scared me witless—mostly because Conrad threw off a rock that whooshed by with a horrifying roar—but today I am above the others and the ropes feel more comfortable. I don't even mind the fearsome fourth pitch, where I unclip from the anchors and swing far into space. My only embarrassment occurs when I knock a small stone squarely onto Mike's helmet. I love arriving at the Sun Deck, and after Mike and I haul up our loads, we lie on our backs, gazing upward at the looming wall and joking about how ridiculous it is for us to be in such a lonely place when it would have been so easy to stay home with our families. We batten down our gear, make sure the ropes are untangled, and rappel back down.

By the time we reach camp, Conrad and Alex have leveled out the kitchen tent floor and thawed our last steaks. Alex is wearing a Santa Claus hat, they've set up a paper Christmas tree, and Bing Crosby is crooning "White Christmas" from a cassette playing in a boom box that Mike brought. We open cards and humorous presents from home. Several of us turn away so others don't see us wipe away tears.

RIGHT: Expedition members celebrate Christmas with humorous gifts from home.

OPPOSITE LEFT TO RIGHT:

Rick Ridgeway after his nose was injured by a falling rock.

Alex Lowe's hands, bloodied from jamming them into cracks.

Conrad Anker watches as Alex Lowe washes his hair. Alex's hygiene drove me crazy; I wanted him to look haggard and battle-weary in my pictures.

Alex Lowe re-leads a difficult, overhanging pitch, 1,200 feet (365 m) above the glacier.

Good climbing photography—and videography—demands enormous cooperation. To complicate matters, it is nearly impossible to work in both mediums at the same time. Inevitably my flash and motor drive ruin Mike's video, and each of us often needs to be in positions that intrude on each other's shots. Furthermore, video often needs to be orchestrated, while stills are best when they are spontaneous. Consequently, Mike and I decide to work one at a time, which means two things: each of us faces long waits in uncomfortable places, and both climbers will need to re-climb their pitches not just once, but twice—each foray as frightening and dangerous as the first. I catch myself questioning the sanity of these compromises Alex and Conrad must make in order to keep their sponsors happy, but recognize that if any one of us had not long ago demonstrated this sort of extra effort, none of us would be climbing Rakekniven.

On the surface, the routine is simple enough. On Alex's overhang pitch, for example, both he and Mike first ascend the rope with ratchet devices (jumars), and then fix a camera line. Next I jumar up and try to hide from view. Then Alex rappels back down to Conrad, who belays as Alex re-climbs the pitch, stopping and starting to meet Mike's storytelling needs. Meanwhile, Mike uses his own line, which he has to hide from his camera, to climb up and down next to Alex. When this is done, Mike hides, Alex rappels back down (taking out his hardware en route), and it's my turn.

CAPTURING THE ACTION

December 28, 1996 (Day 28)

The day after Christmas, we changed our schedule to take better advantage of sunlight (warmth) on the wall. We rise at midnight and try to leave camp by 2 A.M. By this point, Conrad and Alex have led just beyond the halfway point and agree to help Mike and me photograph them re-creating two of the more dramatic pitches, including a fearsome overhang.

OPPOSITE: Jon Krakauer and Conrad Anker (right) set off to establish our hanging camp for the final summit push. Despite hurricane-force winds over nearby peaks, Rakekniven remained mysteriously calm.

Our problem today is that after we have both successfully filmed Alex, Conrad has to clean the overhang pitch so that he has enough hardware to re-lead the following one. This takes longer than expected and by the time Mike finishes filming him on pitch seven, clouds are scudding across the sky. I've been hanging in my harness so long that it feels as if my legs will drop off from lack of circulation, but Conrad has to clean the pitch again. By the time I get started, there is just enough blue sky remaining on the left side of my frame to keep snow and air from blending indistinguishably together. I barely have time to shoot half a dozen rolls before the light goes totally flat.

A HOLE IN MY LIP

January 1, 1997 (Day 32)

Conrad and Alex have now pushed our fixed lines at least 1,600 feet (500 m) above the glacier. It is impossible to climb them each morning and still make significant upward progress, and so it is time to establish a hanging camp. For several days we debated logistics and there is disagreement, albeit friendly, between the climbers (with whom Jon has allied) and the media team. The key question: How much weight can we haul up to the camp? Each additional person means more equipment, food, fuel, and water (which we will take up as ice).

Alex initially suggested that he, Conrad, and Jon should establish the camp alone, finish the climb, and then re-create the adventure for our cameras. When Rick, Mike, and I reject this as fakery, he offers a compromise in which "the media" would continue to live in base camp and jumar up every day to join them. Because this idea would deprive us of key moments that could be critical to our stories (not to mention that it would likely kill the three of us from exertion), we finally agreed to simply haul the weight and move up together. To simplify, however, Conrad suggested that we achieve this in two teams.

Conrad, Jon, and Mike planned to start two days ago, but a mild storm moved in. That cleared yesterday morning, although winds still raged on peaks just south of us, launching snow plumes that stretched hundreds of meters. It would be perilous to be caught in gusts that strong, but Rakekniven seems to be an island free of tempests. By 4 A.M. Conrad's A-team skied away to begin dragging three 100-pound (45 kg) bags up the wall. Two were filled with food and equipment, one with ice.

Now it's our turn, and I quickly learn why Mike calls this "blue-collar climbing." Despite complicated pulley systems that add mechanical advantage and enable a combination of arm strength and body weight to jerk our "pigs" upward, it's still brutal work. "The trick," says Alex, "is to swear a lot!"

The worst part, especially low on the route, is that the bags inevitably snag on all protuberances. Someone has to jumar below and drag them free. They also knock rocks loose. Before I am 300 feet (100 m) off the deck, I look up at just the wrong moment. A stone no bigger than a film can, one that should have bounced harmlessly off my helmet, slams straight into my lower lip,

As I hang 1,200 feet (365 m) above the glacier, the cliff below my feet is so steep that if I drop a roll of film, it would hit the snow without once bouncing off the rock.

Alex Lowe relaxes on a portaledge, 1,700 feet (520 m) above the glacier.

nearly punching my incisors straight through it. Blood pours down my chin and my tongue feels a gaping hole. I wonder if the climb is over for me.

Nevertheless, I hear Alex yelling. Apparently I need to free the lowest bag, and so I persevere upward. By the time I rejoin Rick on the Sun Deck, he tells me that my wound "doesn't look that bad," and after studying it in my camera's tiny shutter mirror, I decide to go on.

Alex, the strongest person any of us has ever encountered, decides to speed our progress by providing all the muscle. I'm awestruck watching him jumar pitch after pitch as gracefully as a monkey on a vine. Rick volunteers to free any snagged pigs, and because I am obviously in mild shock, constantly exploring my wound with my tongue, they tell me simply to get myself up to camp. The rest of the day is a blur as I ascend one seemingly endless rope after another. At least the cliff is now so overhanging that Rick's job is easy, and I realize that if I drop anything it won't even bounce before hitting the snow below. My biggest problem is dizziness, triggered because I cannot touch any rock to stop myself from spinning.

Gordon Wiltsie photographing just below the summit. PHOTO BY RICK RIDGEWAY

THE HANGING CAMP

January 2, 1997 (Day 33)

I have never before slept on a portaledge and I am astonished by my comfort, even when it rocks back and forth. My only complaint is that I share mine with Alex, whose mischievous mind is at the opposite end. When he thinks that I'm unaware, he sometimes abruptly steps outside, unweighting the tent like a kid jumping off a teeter-totter. I'm still anchored to the wall in my harness, but it is horrifying to flip into a headstand, staring straight down to the glacier 1,400 feet (425 m) below.

Today's first lead goes to Conrad, who leaves his sleeping bag at about 2 A.M. and climbs sideways for about 100 feet (30 m) before rounding a corner and disappearing from sight. The first part is tricky free climbing, followed by periodically difficult aid. The 200-foot (60 m) pitch takes five hours, and then Jon starts up the rope to lead the next one. In deference to his remarkable mountaineering skills, which he always understates in his writing, we all want him to lead at least one pitch on this climb, his first since Everest. Unknown to us, this pitch involves very technical, time-consuming tool placements. By noon, Alex has long since straightened out every rope, boiled water for all our bottles, and tried in vain to read. He simply cannot stand still.

He radios Conrad to suggest that he should zoom up to take over after Jon is finished and continue climbing into the "night." Unfortunately, Jon's pitch remains difficult and by the time he sets up a belay it is already 3 P.M. The sun is about to disappear, and Alex's plan doesn't make sense. Nevertheless, he still climbs up to lead one more devious section past loose, knife-edged flakes before rapelling back to relax with a brief night's sleep.

OPPOSITE: Conrad Anker free climbs out of our hanging camp as Jon Krakauer belays.

OPPOSITE: Conrad Anker re-leads a pitch out of our hanging camp as Jon Krakauer belays and Mike Graber films.

BELOW: Alex Lowe and Conrad Anker embrace as Jon Krakauer joins them on the summit snowfield.

THE LAST HEADWALL

January 3, 1997 (Day 34)

Alex lights the stove at 1 A.M. and begins melting ice. He is slated to jumar first, followed quickly by Rick, who will belay his next lead. Within an hour Alex is harnessed and laced into his climbing shoes. "Have you got an ETD yet?" he calls down to Rick's portaledge. I pity Rick and Mike, who I imagine are scurrying to coordinate both Rick's departure and Mike's shooting schedule. "No hurry," Alex continues, obviously trying to keep impatience from his tone. "I'm just wondering when to start!"

Once Rick and Alex depart, the rest of us relax until the sun appears. Mike and I trade off filming Conrad re-leading the pitch out of camp in beautiful morning light. Despite my lip wound, I actually enjoy jumaring pitches eleven and twelve, even if the first begins with a complicated traverse. Then I face the wildest stretch of all, pitch thirteen, where a solitary rope hangs in space, meters away from the whitest, blankest granite we have seen so far. Looking through my camera, I'm astonished by the contrast between vertical rock and flat, horizontal ice cap that stretches to the horizon below. I can scarcely believe my good fortune as I watch Conrad ascend ahead of me. In this single frame, everything good about the climb comes together: a tiny climber dangles high above the glacier, a pinpoint sun perfectly positioned to electrify the scene. I twist my aperture down to f/22 to turn it into a star. A view like this, I think, is the reason that I climb.

Seldom have I more fully enjoyed ascending a rope. I revel in the vast emptiness below my feet and feel I am the luckiest person alive. I'm much stronger than I was in Cape Town, and I quickly pull myself over the edge, sneak past a series of razor-edged flakes, and join my companions below one last overhang. Alex has already overcome it and Mike is leading the last few moves above it.

Our emotions run high, but the summit is visually anticlimactic. Once we're over the vertical edge, we encounter a snow slope that seamlessly blends into the glacier far below, as if there were no cliff at all. Nevertheless, Alex bolts forward to embrace Conrad in a bear hug and we all join elbows to stagger the last few feet. Then, out of nowhere, Alex almost ruins our day.

"We're not the first to climb this!" he gasps, trying to keep a straight face. He points to our feet, where we see tiny tracks. "I guess the first ascent really belongs to a bird," he says. "Why don't we call it the Snow Petrel Wall?"

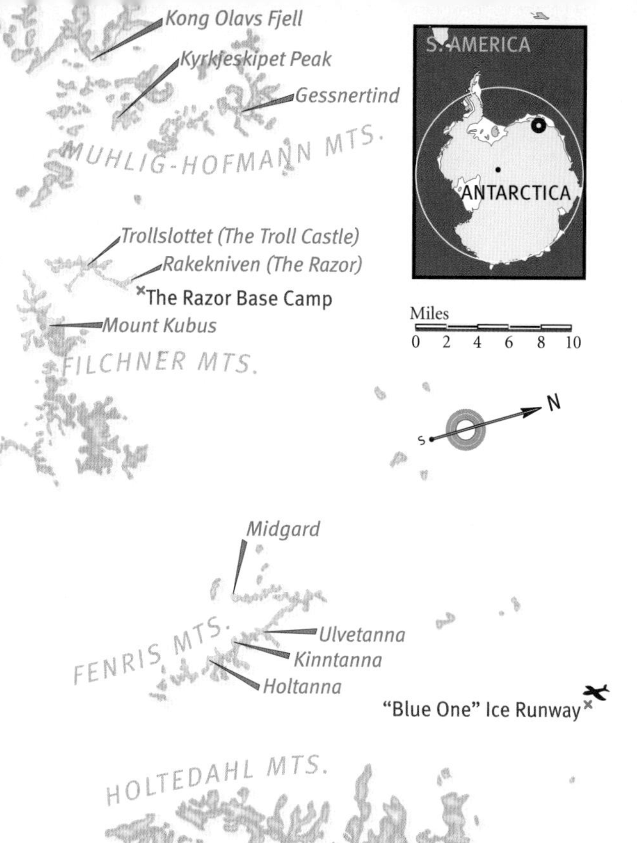

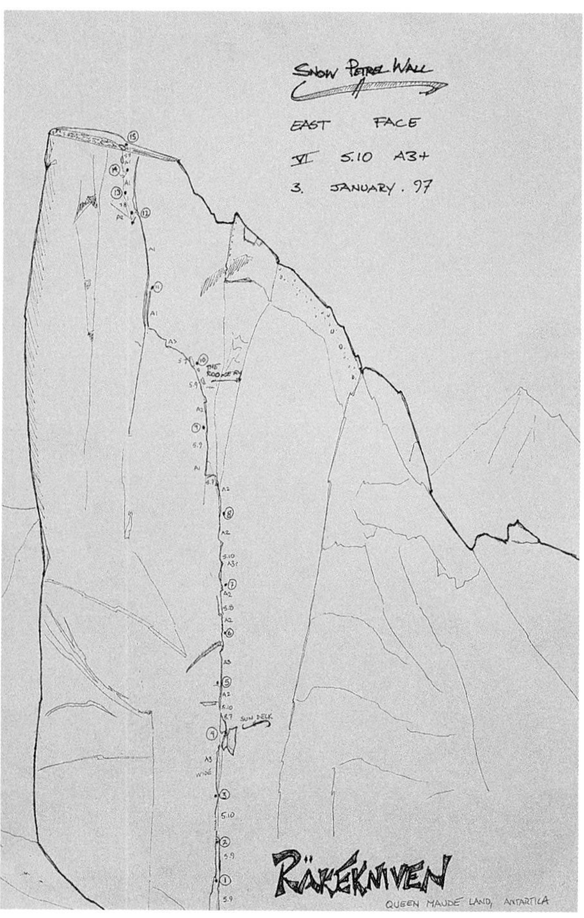

A climber's "topo" map of the Snow Petrel Wall drawn by Conrad Anker.

Conrad Anker leads difficult free climbing on Troll's Castle while Jon Krakauer belays and Alex Lowe takes pictures.

THE TROLL'S CASTLE

January 14, 1997 (Day 35)

Like a cuckoo clock, Alex wakes precisely at midnight. "It's a beautiful day!" he shouts. "Let's get after it!" After one failed attempt and several other intermediate skiing, kite-flying, and ski-parachuting adventures, today is our last chance to climb the Troll's Castle, a prominent spire behind Rakekniven. The Twin Otter is scheduled to pick us up tomorrow.

A week ago, our first attempt did not go well. Bored by several days of storms, Alex convinced us to bolt for the peak as soon as the weather appeared to be propitious. The crag looked like a modest, though potentially difficult, day climb, but by the time we had ascended the glacier a thousand or so vertical feet (350 m) to the Castle's base, it was midafternoon and shadows were creeping across our route. Alex suggested we bivouac and wait until the sun reemerged. Within hours everyone regretted our decision. No sooner did the sun disappear than the temperature plummeted below 10°F (–17°C) and the wind picked up. While the others scurried back and forth, searching for patches of sun, I stuffed my legs into my rucksack, made a pillow from coiled ropes, and tried to sleep. But every time I dozed off, dreaming of distant, far-more-pleasant places, someone rudely shook me, fearing that I was dying from hypothermia. By morning all of us were so exhausted that we retreated.

Alex Lowe and Mike Graber endure a bivouac on Troll's Castle.

Today we hope that things will go better. We quickly reach a col between Troll's Castle and a satellite spire with a snowy ridge that looks much easier to ascend. Because it will be more efficient to climb the difficult peak with a smaller team, we agree that Conrad, Alex, and Jon will attempt Troll's Castle, while the rest of us photograph them from its neighbor, which we jokingly dub Media Peak.

The day is magical, with two teams of friends each climbing a virgin mountain via a magnificent route. On Troll's Castle, Alex leads an easy first pitch up huge rock pockets called huecos, and then Conrad forges up the hardest free climbing anyone has done during the entire expedition. From the Castle, our route up Media Peak looks almost as spectacular. Despite an awkward, poorly protected rock step that Rick bulls right through, we reach the top much earlier than they do and shoot Conrad striding up a last snowfield to the summit pinnacle, where he is silhouetted against a vast polar plateau that stretches all the way to the pole.

By eight o'clock we're back at base camp, exhausted but exuberant about a perfect cap to an already superlative journey. We agree that this has been the best expedition of our lives.

OPPOSITE: Alex Lowe rappels off Troll's Castle; Media Peak is in the background.

The expedition caravan follows an ancient Inca trail through pastures above our starting point at Unamen.

CHAPTER SEVEN

LOST TOMBS OF THE ANCIENTS

Sleuthing Pre-Incan Secrets, Rio Huabayacu, Peru, 1999

- ***Location:*** Rio Huabayacu in La Libertad District, Peru; 7° S, 76° W; approximately 30 miles (50 km) south-southeast of Leymebamba, in cloud forests of the upper Amazon basin
- ***Team:*** Peter Lerche, John Catto, Maria Montoya Vera, Gordon Wiltsie
- ***Dates:*** October 23 to November 9, 1999, round-trip from Lima
- ***Conditions:*** Mixed sun, rain, and fog, with temperatures between 30°F (−1°C) and 75°F (24°C)

LATE IN AUGUST 1999, *Adventure* magazine assigned me to photograph a guided horseback trip into remote, but inhabited, cloud forests and high grasslands of the northern Andes. Our leader was German-born archaeologist Dr. Peter Lerche, who had spent two decades studying the Chachapoyans, a mysterious pre-Incan culture. Little is known about them, except that they were such fierce warriors that when the Inca conquered them in the 1400s, many played key roles in the Inca's subsequent battles with the Spanish.

For me, the highlight of our journey was exploring Kuelap, an ancient Chachapoyan fortress. Huge stone walls that Peter said contained almost as much rock as the giant pyramid at Giza protected an ancient, mountain-top town that was nearly half a mile (1 km) long and at least 300 feet (100 m) wide. Much of the site has been reconstructed by the Peruvian National Cultural Institute (INC), and it was as impressive as Macchu Picchu. I couldn't believe I had never heard of it before.

Based on this ignorance, which I assumed was widespread, I thought a story about Kuelap and the Chachapoyans would interest *National Geographic* readers. Over breakfast after our return to the modern town of Chachapoyas, I suggested to Peter that we collaborate. "Yes. That would be interesting," he whispered, looking over his shoulder to see if anyone was listening, "but I know of something better."

OPPOSITE: Kuelap, an ancient, pre-Incan fortress built by the Chachapoyans, a culture that thrived in the northern cloud forests of Peru's upper Amazon basin.

OPPOSITE: An *arriero* leads his mount over a rocky pass in grasslands above the Rio Yonan.

The Chachapoyans, he told me, often built cliff-side tombs for their leaders, which are scattered throughout the jungle. "But every time an archaeologist gets to one, it has already been looted. I think that I have found one that is still pristine."

I called *National Geographic* editors Peter Miller and Bert Fox as soon as I returned home, and they were intrigued. Because there was no guarantee of success, however, they suggested that Lerche and I travel to the tomb on reconnaissance first. Then, if it actually was unmolested, we could obtain permits to return, excavate the site, and then leave everything *in situ,* protected in some manner that would discourage looters.

Meanwhile, Maryanne Culpepper, the director of story development for the *National Geographic Explorer* television program, also expressed interest, and asked us to include John Catto to film me working on assignment. No matter what we found, she would have a story, and if the site was undisturbed, so much the better. Now we just had to outrace both looters and the rainy season.

A carving on a cornerstone block of a sun temple at Kuelap.

THE INCA "HIGHWAY"

October 26, 1999 (Day 4)

"*¡Caramba!*" I hear from just behind me on the trail. Sensing a picture, I dash back and see that one of our packhorses slipped on a muddy rock slab and tumbled 100 feet (30 m) down a precipitous slope into a thicket of bamboo and thorns. Its feet are kicking wildly in the air, but the load prevents it from standing back up.

Two of the *arrieros,* horsemen, scramble down to free the beast. It appears to be unharmed—probably because the ground is so sodden. We resume our travel and soon the overgrown trail goes from bad to terrible. In many places we have to hop from stone to stone to avoid miring up to our knees in mud. Huge tropical hardwoods tower overhead and long, moss-covered vines, hosting an occasional orchid, hang down. At times we can scarcely find the route and simply grope from one slippery tree root to the next. I can't believe that any horse can fight its way through this terrain, or that our route used to be a major Incan thoroughfare.

The going is bad enough for Peter, John, and me, but it is far worse for Peter's cousin by marriage, Maria Montoya Vera, a graduate student in archaeology from Trujillo University. She has never before ridden a horse, battled such treacherous footing, or even camped. She is terrified and constantly leans on Peter for physical support.

I reflect back on the astonishing environmental changes we have experienced since morning, when we awoke at Inca Pirca. Surrounded by high, foggy grasslands, our marshy campsite was set beside a ruined guesthouse that likely served the leading Incan highway to Ecuador. At first our route was paved with stones, but after less than an hour it plummeted into a canyon formed by the Rio Yonan, a tributary to the Huabayacu. Jungle instantly surrounded us.

After an interminable descent, we finally encounter the river and my mood changes from grim resignation to wonder. Crystal-clear water tumbles between mossy rocks overhung by tree trunks that are festooned with lichens, flowers, and mushrooms. I see trout dart from one rill to another and curse myself for not bringing a fishing pole. Despite the rain and mud, and the bushes that slap my face, this stream enchants me with its microcosmic beauty, bubbling through the forest.

Peter Lerche drinks from the Rio Yonan, not far from Pampa Hermosa.

AN UNEXPECTED ENTOURAGE

October 27, 1999 (Day 5)

We wake in Pampa Hermosa, a single-family "village," where our guide Maximilliano Siccha and his son Mario have cleared and burned a few hundred acres of virgin forest for their increasing cattle herd. Our cook, Alfonso, bought fresh eggs and I flirt playfully with Mario's young wife, who is afraid of my camera. Rain that poured all night finally stopped and John and I lounge in warm sun, watching a rooster guard his harem.

Settled safely back home at a Sierra Club meeting, I'd be outraged by these people who are destroying our planetary rain forests. But what am I to do? Lecture them? Indeed, Maximilliano and his family are the very kind of rugged individualists who tamed the American West. If they had not hacked out a place in the jungle, they'd be living in a slum in Chiclayo, sewing sandals for a dollar a day—assuming that any one of them could find a job. Instead, they now have a few score head of cattle. How can I blame them?

Although Peter wants to forge ahead this morning, Mario tells him that "visitors" are coming. As if carried by jungle drums, word travels quickly here, and Peter already seems to know who they will be. Around noon, four no-nonsense-looking men stride up to the hut and greet Peter as if he is an old friend, albeit one not to be completely trusted. All are from La Morada, a recently established hamlet several days march on overgrown trails down the Rio Huabayacu, along which we are now camped.

Peter introduces them: Juan Guerrero, a Seventh-day Adventist pastor, Antonio Floríndez

OPPOSITE: The homestead at Pampa Hermosa, which was burned from the cloud forests of the Rio Yonan Valley

Homesteader Maximilliano Siccha attends a salt lick he has built for his cattle, which graze in fields he has burned out of the cloud forests.

Untol, the regional governor, and Jose Eloy Rojas Peche, Antonio's adjutant. The most intimidating is Zacarias Añazco Bardales, a son from the first marriage of Don Benigno Añazco, a legendary pioneer. Zacarias' father is reported to believe he is on a mission from God to populate the cloud forests. Wild stories about him abound, but most people agree that after establishing several farms, he divorced his first wife, blasted his son-in-law point-blank with a shotgun to keep him from running drugs, and currently is hiding deep in the jungle with his daughter, who has borne him several children.

I ask Peter why these men have appeared and he tells me, "They are the closest thing to the law in this part of Peru, and they think we are going to rob the tombs."

LOOK, BUT DON'T TOUCH

October 31, 1999 (Day 9)

"The tomb is unlooted!" shouts Peter, his voice ringing with ecstasy. John, who rappelled first to film him, has already suggested this, but Peter's learned eyes confirm it. I rush to snap my own rappel device onto the line and head over the brushy edge, where mud, weeds, and small stones pour down around me.

As I descend into space I can finally see through the open roof of this structure we have dubbed "the White House." Inside are several bundles, each wrapped in coarse, ancient cloth, outside of which are wooden slats, and finally a tight winding of thick, hand-braided rope. Beside the bundles are propped a prehistoric spear and a copper-headed mace that

Maximilliano Siccha and his family in Unamen.

would be almost priceless on the black market—proving that no robbers have visited the site. The tomb, carefully constructed on a sloping ledge several hundred feet (100 m) up a vertical cliff, sheltered by an overhang, is painted white. Deer antlers are stuck between stones on either side of an open door. Two red circles that Peter says probably symbolize eyes are painted on the cliff behind. Because everything is set in such a precarious place, with no ledges leading to it from any direction, I wonder how the Chachapoyans built it. I also wonder why nothing has rotted.

Even though we first sighted the tomb three days ago, reaching it has proved to be an epic quest. After establishing a base camp at a small farm owned by Hernán Borges, we spent a full day chopping our way through sometimes-vertical forests to a dense brushy area somewhere above the White House. Although anchors were difficult to find (even big trees were so shallowly rooted that they could be toppled by body weight), John established a line and began to rappel through the bushes, being careful not to slice through his rope as he wielded a razor-sharp machete to clear a path to cliff's edge. To our dismay, however, he descended at least 100 feet (35 m) too far east and couldn't even see the tomb. By the time he climbed back up and found new anchors in a better place, it was too dark to proceed. Our sole consolation was finding another, unexpected burial site hidden in a cave. Unfortunately, nothing remained except for a skull and a few human bones. Everything else had

FAR LEFT: The White House tomb, on a cliff above Rio Huabayacu, appears to be accessible only by rappelling, a skill the ancient Chachapoyans probably had not perfected.

LEFT: John Catto hacks through dense brush before rappelling in his first attempt to reach the tomb. With every swing, he had to be vigilant that his machete did not sever the rope!

BELOW: John Catto crawls through thick undergrowth en route to the White House. Many vines looked like snakes, and I took comfort from my ignorance about the presence of any poisonous varieties.

We found this looted tomb in a cave hidden in the jungle near the White House. There was no clue about which century it was plundered, nor where any of the artifacts have gone—a widespread phenomena that leaves many mysteries about Chachapoyan culture.

been taken—a bad omen for the White House, Peter thought.

Yesterday it rained so hard we could barely make it partway up the hill above base camp before turning back. Even coca couldn't motivate our crew. By that point the forest was giving me the creeps. Every few steps I had to grab a vine, many of which looked like snakes. Would one of them be a deadly fer-de-lance? I was afraid to ask if they frequented these parts. Further complicating matters, Peter had never climbed before. John and I gave him rudimentary rappelling and jumaring lessons on a boulder at Pampa Hermosa, but all of us wonder how he will fare when he is dangling in midair, hundreds of feet off the ground under an overhang. Getting down will be easy, but can he make it back up?

Those hardships are now forgotten. Peter is sufficiently jubilant that he easily overcomes his fear. He is admittedly clumsy at the mechanical tasks of using our hardware, but also strong enough to make up for any lack of experience. For more than two hours we take turns ratcheting up and down one of the two ropes we have fixed, each of us doing our jobs. As Peter examines every detail of the tomb, I take pictures of him, and John films both of us.

Our one genuine disappointment is that our official permit states that we can only take photographs. We are not allowed to touch the tomb, much less scrape away a foot-deep (30 cm) layer of leaves that might be hiding any manner of treasure. Even if we are tempted, I know that Zacarias and his crew—to whom I have loaned my spare camera and 400mm lens—are watching us from the opposite hill.

THE LOST TEMPLE

November 1, 1999 (Day 10)

Yesterday evening, after we returned from the White House, Hernán described to Peter a strange place he had found while searching for a stray cow. It looked like an ancient temple, he said, and he sketched out a pattern that was repeated in the masonry. Immediately Peter asked him to take us there.

Our entourage leaves early, at first following a tumbling stream that we must ford. Then Hernán bears straight uphill, his machete flying through tangled vines, bamboo, and other impediments. Within an hour he stops beside a large rock and proudly hoists the remnants of a big, earthen pot. Soon thereafter we encounter manmade rock walls that appear to separate ancient farming terraces. Then we see the circular walls of a house. As if to warn us away, one of the stones is carved into an eerie likeness of a human face.

As we look more closely around us, the outlines of other structures, long-since swallowed by the jun-

OPPOSITE: Peter Lerche examines the White House after rappelling to it from above. This was his first-ever experience with such climbing techniques. Note the deer antler stuck into the whitewashed stones and the mummy bundle perched in the doorway.

Peter Lerche studies mummy bundles inside the White House. An ancient mace and spear are propped in the corner—priceless artifacts that prove the tomb was unlooted. Sadly, we did not have a permit to touch anything inside, much less clear away leaves to see what lay beneath.

gle, appear in the undergrowth. Hernán leads us to what must have been this prehistoric city's center—a massive, virtually intact circular wall, probably 60 feet (20 m) in diameter. Stone crosses are inset at eye level all the way around. Peter has never before seen a Chachapoyan ruin with these shapes. Even our new friends from La Morada are awed, and we are all strangely quiet as we wander through the trees, encountering new structures every few steps.

"I have found many things in the cloud forests," says Peter, "but this is one of the most impressive. At some point in history, this must have been a major population center." He studies the strange crosses at length, as if they hold the key to a deeper mystery—the as-yet-unknown religious practices of the Chachapoyans. "This place needs a name," he says. "Why don't we call it Chacana Llajta?" This Quechua moniker means "city of the crosses" and is pronounced *chacana yahkta.*

I feel like Indiana Jones.

JEALOUSY AND DECEPTION

Follow-up, August 18, 2000

■ ***Location:*** Lima, Peru, 12° S, 77° W

"Ben," I tell my sixteen-year-old son, "it's midnight and time for me to go to the police station. Here are five thousand dollars, your passport, and your plane ticket home. If I'm not back by morning, take a taxi straight to the airport, call Mom, and catch the first flight."

This is not the ending I had planned for our first assignment together. Just two weeks earlier we had been brimming with excitement for a follow-up expe-

Peter Lerche examines carving on a nailstone, a common feature of Chachapoyan structures.

dition to the White House with Peter. To my surprise, the editors at *National Geographic* had been so excited about our earlier discoveries that they wanted to avoid being scooped and had laid out a story without the excavation and preservation components we had originally planned. Before the article hit the newsstands in September, everyone agreed that we had to finish the mission to protect the White House from looting. Because television was no longer involved and we still needed a second experienced climber, I brought Ben (who could already climb better than me) in place of John.

We left the States assured that all permits were in place. In fact, the wife of President Fujimori's cousin (a top presidential advisor who was acting as our liaison with the government) was coming with us as an adventure travel holiday. Before we could begin loading any horses, however, we started hitting snags. For some reason the INC director would not okay our permit. Even after *National Geographic* sent an advance copy of the Chachapoyan story to the first lady (who is Fujimori's daughter, not his wife), we could make no progress.

Then Peter learns through a cousin of his own (everything official seems to happen via "cousins" here) that a policeman who is the business partner of an amateur archaeologist, sun-worshipper, and travel guide from Reno, Nevada, filed official paperwork "denouncing" Peter, Maria, and me for grave robbery. Although anyone can denounce anyone else for virtually anything, it is the official first step toward arrest, after which we would be considered guilty until proven innocent. Without clearing the *denuncia,* Peter's cousin says, we'll get no permit.

OPPOSITE: Ben Wiltsie, bored and frustrated in a café in Chachapoyas, where we waited long days for the National Cultural Institute to approve a permit for us to secure the White House tomb.

To avoid interrogation at a police station in Saposoa, a long day's bus ride deeper into the Amazon, I pay for an officer to fly to Lima, where Ben, Peter, Maria, and I will join him. The moment of truth is upon us.

I hug Ben goodbye, and the rest of us ride a taxi about half an hour through ever-seedier neighborhoods. We stop at a dilapidated concrete building, where we are ushered into a whitewashed room with a desk, battered old typewriter, stack of carbon paper, and a poster of Macchu Picchu with the headline WELCOME TO PERU. A police colonel greets us and shakes hands warmly with Peter, as if this is just a charade. One by one we sit down as he and the officer from Saposoa ask questions that we answer either *"si"* or *"no."* The colonel hunts and pecks every word in triplicate.

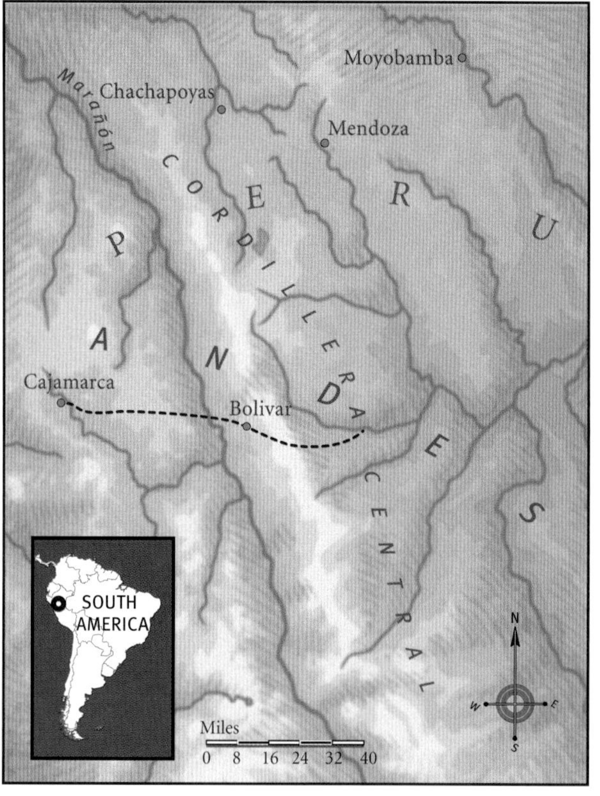

I am very worried, but thanks to Peter's foresight, all of our original companions from La Morada had provided him with hand-written documents—stamped with multiple official seals—stating that they had observed our every move and that we had committed no crimes. Peter has these with him, and they are enough to convince the colonel. *"Bueno,"* he says. We sign all the copies he has typed, notarize them with our thumbprints, and prepare to leave.

Then, however, an unctuous man who has been lurking in the background comes forward. "The colonel is wrong," he says. "This case is still in many files. I am a lawyer, and you need my help to make them go away." I know that he sees me as a potential hostage with *National Geographic* pockets behind me, and so I insist he tell me how much that is going to cost. By late the next afternoon, a courier hands me a letter from the lawyer. My case is serious and will take much time, it states. For that reason, his fees will be $150,000, with a $50,000 retainer due immediately. I imagine that he is already at the police station, arranging my imminent arrest. Without stopping to think, Ben and I pack our bags and head straight to the airport. I pray that there is not already an alert for my name at customs, but no one stops us and we board our plane. I only relax, however, after I hear the wheels leave the tarmac.

Only later did we learn that many of our troubles were rooted in the imminent collapse of President Fujimori's government, after which he and his top officals (including our liaison and his wife) fled the country themselves.

OPPOSITE: Zacarias Añazco Bardales holds the stamp with which he, the regional governor, and others certified a letter stating that we had committed no wrongs while investigating the White House. Peter Lerche requested this document, which seemed unimportant to me until the day it kept us out of jail.

CHAPTER EIGHT

A MONTH ON A POLAR WALL

Great Sail Peak, Baffin Island, Canada, 1998

ABOVE: Mount Asgard, Auyuittuq National Park.

OPPOSITE: Jared Ogden aid climbs high on the upper wall.

- ***Location:*** The Sail Peaks, Stewart Valley, Baffin Island; 71° N; 71° W; 293 miles (472 km) north of the Arctic Circle
- ***Team:*** Greg Child (leader), Alex Lowe, Jared Ogden, Mark Synnott, Gordon Wiltsie, and *National Geographic* videographer John Catto
- ***Dates:*** May 16 to June 30, 1998, from my arrival in Clyde River, Nunavut, until our return
- ***Conditions:*** Widely varied, ranging from blizzards with winds over 60 mph (100 kph) and temperatures as low as –20°F (–30°C) to sunny with temperatures above 40°F (5°C) and no wind. During the span of the expedition, a lake that was frozen with more than 8 feet (2.5 m) of ice completely thawed.

THE SOARING STONE MONOLITHS of Canada's remote Baffin Island first gained international attention when climber Rick Sylvester ski-jumped thousands of feet off Mount Asgard in Auyuittuq National Park, working as a James Bond stuntman in the opening sequence of *The Spy Who Loved Me.* The astonishing scene, which is supposed to be set in Austria, defies credibility, but as Bond's Union Jack parachute unfurls, the camera zooms back to reveal a jaw-dropping landscape.

ABOVE LEFT: Greg Child in −30°F (−22°C) temperatures below Great Sail Peak during a scouting expedition.

BELOW LEFT: Mark Synnott aboard a ski plane during our exploratory flight.

For cutting-edge mountaineers Auyuittuq was just the beginning of a new frontier. After the most obvious and aesthetic lines in the park were climbed, some looked northward to cliffs between the Inuit hamlets of Clyde River and Pond Inlet—a landscape strewn with granite monuments equivalent to Yosemite's legendary Half Dome or El Capitan. Among these pioneers was Mark Synnott, a young mountaineer from New Hampshire who first visited the island in May and June 1995 and then came back a year later. Together with several companions, he climbed three huge towers. The culmination of their trip was a twenty-five-day ascent of Polar Sun Spire, a 4,400 vertical foot (1,350 m), mostly overhanging cliff above Sam Ford Fjord. Many considered it the longest, hardest polar big wall ever done. Any sane person would have moved on. But Mark dreamed of even higher, more difficult Baffin walls.

Mark shared his thoughts with a few friends, including Greg Child, an Australian-American climbing star famed for entertaining prose about his epics around the world. By coincidence, the editors at *National Geographic* wanted Greg to write an expedition story for them. After the popular success of the piece Jon Krakauer and I had done in Queen Maud Land, they were intrigued by a northern counterpart and gave Greg an assignment. Greg and Mark were sponsored by The North Face, the company agreed to share the cost, and two other members of their climbing team quickly joined the expedition: Alex Lowe and Jared Ogden, a young mountaineer who had just teamed with Mark to climb a massive face in Pakistan.

Even though Mark, Jared, and Greg could take good pictures, *National Geographic* also wanted to send a photographer who had worked previously for the magazine and knew how to create the not-so-obvious storytelling images the editors always need. After the Queen Maud Land expedition (see chapter 6), I was an obvious choice. Finally, National Geographic Television added John Catto to shoot video for their series, *Explorer.*

Only one serious question remained. *Which* mountain were we going to climb? Mark had a couple of ideas, things he had heard about, but hadn't actually *seen* anything that topped, or even equaled, Polar

OPPOSITE: Great Sail Peak and saxifrage flowers after the spring thaw.

Sun Spire. That made Bert Fox, my illustrations editor at *National Geographic*, seriously nervous. The Society was preparing to spend close to $100,000 on a very big "if." To help us find the most spectacular possible crag, he suggested that he join us for an exploratory flight the length of Baffin, which is nearly as big as California. Our expedition was born.

THE VIEW FROM ABOVE

April 3, 1998 (pre-expedition)

Bert's idea was brilliant. While flying up and down Baffin, we see more towering monoliths than we can remember. Each promises different complexities and panoramas, and we argue about which looks best. We return to a wall of crags we spotted early in the morning. Our map calls them Sail Peaks.

Alex beams with delight as our ski-equipped Twin Otter circles these seemingly blank, overhanging massifs—some of the biggest and scariest cliffs I have ever seen. Our altimeter gauges the tallest to be even loftier than Mark's previous climbs, and as our pilot banks straight above it, I am engulfed by vertigo.

We land on a frozen lake. The Sail Peaks glow in the setting sun, and we have to crane our necks to see their summits. Alex, Greg, and Mark quickly decide we have found our goal, and plot hypothetical routes that are invisible to me. Jared, who was unable to accompany the scouting flight, would have to take their decision on faith.

OPPOSITE: Inuit hunter Jayko Apak, equipped with a traditional harpoon, waits on an ice floe for a ringed seal to appear.

But there is just one problem. The temperature is –30°F (–22°C). With only a month to go before departure, will it be warm enough for anyone to remove their gloves to hold pitons or snuggle cams into icy cracks?

SEAL HUNTING

May 26, 1998 (Day 11)

In order to reach the climb, we planned to work with Inuit guides, whose snowmobiles could drag us in kamatik sleds piled with our gear. They thought the journey to base camp from Clyde River (which we reached in an overloaded plane) would take three or four days. Between storms and breakdowns, however, we're now already into the fifth, with a long way to go. Just last night, a screaming blizzard almost blew away our tents, and when it cleared, the new snow was too deep and soft for the snowmobiles. We have to wait until at least 10 P.M., when our head guide, Jushua Illuaq, thinks the surface will solidify.

ABOVE: Young Inuit guide Romeo Palluq.

BELOW: Romeo Palluq teases Alex Lowe, who is working out during a stormbound stay at a hunter's cabin near Clyde River.

FOLLOWING SPREAD, LEFT: John Catto stands in the window of a hunter's cabin, where the expedition was stuck for three days by a blizzard.

FOLLOWING SPREAD, RIGHT: The expedition parks atop a pass between Sam Ford Fjord and Stewart Valley while Inuit guides repair a snowmobile.

Inuit guide Jayko Apak works on an ice hole he chopped through lake ice for fishing and fresh water.

Jayko Apak and Laimake Pulluq invite me to join them for a brief hunt. Several ringed seals are dozing beside their breathing holes and we pursue them—first by snowmobile, then on foot, behind white camouflage shields. Despite several shots, they all escape. We only capture a tiny fish that one seal had intended to eat. I feel grateful to glimpse my companions' deep roots to the land and sea.

AN ARCTIC YOSEMITE

May 29, 1998 (Day 14)

As we motor into the eerie Stewart Valley, shrouded in subzero mist, I can imagine how John Muir felt when he first glimpsed Yosemite Valley. This is a landscape of the gods, bordered by impregnable stone abutments. Only the Sail Peaks have a name. All of us are elated to be in base camp, but our objective looms menacingly overhead. Worse, it's still so cold that we need gloves, and all of us are worried about the jam cracks and friction holds above.

Our Inuit friends think we're insane. Not one has even entered the Stewart Valley before. Legends say that it's not a place to find caribou, geese, or other game. Still, Jayko chops through 8 feet (2.5 m) of lake ice, hoping to catch a fish, or at least to give us a watering hole. After three hours of jigging a lure he gets nary a strike, and the water is too silty to drink.

TORRENTS OF ROCK AND WATER

June 6, 1998 (Day 22)

After days of tortuous route-finding through loose flakes, overhangs, and tenuous cracks, Greg, Alex,

OPPOSITE: Alex Lowe sits atop a boulder above base camp after stringing Tibetan Buddhist prayer flags to bless the team

Mark Synnott ferries a load to the base of the wall. The fog below was so thick that I almost didn't take my camera that day.

LEFT: An expedition member ascends a 600-foot (185 m) free-hanging rope below the huge ledge that splits the north face of Great Sail Peak.

Mark, and Jared have fixed ropes to a huge ledge a third of the way up the wall. Anyone who isn't climbing ferries load after load of food and equipment—at least a ton—a thousand vertical feet (300 m) to the base of the climb. It's a miserable, backbreaking task, during which we often wallow through deep snow that is barely glued to slippery rock slabs. At last we are ready to leave the ground behind.

I'm eager to get above this dangerous lower section. Temperatures have risen dramatically and snowmelt on the ledge is washing stones of all sizes down our route. Two "nights" ago we watched a slab as big as a Cadillac exfoliate from the wall. It bounded so far that it nearly reached the lake. Even scarier, four days ago, while I was photographing Alex and Greg leading overhead, enough rocks to fill a dump truck tumbled straight toward us. Alex and Greg were safely under an overhang, but I had nowhere to run. I felt like a duck beset by bird shot and emerged traumatized, my feet ringed by craters made by missiles that should have killed me.

But there are lighter moments, too. Yesterday morning the snow started melting so fast in base camp that Jared woke up floating in a creek. Without frenzied trenching and dike-building, almost every other tent would have been washed away. Spring has arrived.

OPPOSITE: Alex Lowe and Mark Synnott attempt to establish radio contact from Ledge Camp to our Inuit support crew in Clyde River. The frozen lake in Stewart Valley is below.

Jared Ogden looks mournfully at a snowmelt stream that began to flow under his tent as he slept.

Alex Lowe shaves in base camp. As with the Queen Maud Expedition, this frustrated me because it made him look too clean-cut for the camera.

LEFT: Alex Lowe leads very difficult aid climbing. Here he balances in rope slings suspended by multiple weak anchors (including pitons stacked together) that are equalized with the slings to share his body weight.

typical placement is something like a 1/16-inch-thick (2 mm) "stopper," tied together with slings and carabiners to other miscellaneous pitons that are themselves stacked atop each other and hammered barely 1/4 inch (8 mm) into a crack the thickness of my fingernail. One body length at a time, he follows this with another similarly insane perch, until he is far above Mark's belay, still going strong.

ALPINE ENGINEERING

June 11, 1998 (Day 27)

We're into the swing of it now, with two-man teams exchanging leads almost twenty-four hours a day. But it's slow going. Some days it takes a dozen hours to climb just 200 feet (60 m). I spend the evening with Mark and Alex, watching Alex lead a pitch he calls Eye of the Storm. Every inch of upward progress requires creative engineering, and I am astonished by the precarious tools to which he attaches his sling ladders. A

RIGHT: Mark Synnott dozes during a ten-hour belay as Alex Lowe inches his way upward.

It seems to me that if he so much as sneezes, any one of the tenuous placements could rip loose, launching him into a fall that would zipper everything loose and send him flying for hundreds of vertical feet. Given modern technology, very stretchy ropes, and a complete absence of ledges to hit, however, this might not even hurt. Theoretically Mark—who is anchored to the cliff with bombproof anchors—would catch him with a friction device, and all would be well. Furthermore, our belay tools are semiautomatic, which means that they feed out rope if it is pulled slowly, but lock tightly if jerked. This proves to be very important when—as happens to many of our team—Mark becomes so bored from belaying through a ten-hour lead that he falls asleep.

DANCING FOR THE CAMERA

June 15, 1998 (Day 31)

Our nonstop climbing is exhausting me. We are on a north-facing wall, so the sun, which never sets, appears about three in the afternoon and swings back behind the cliff about twelve hours later. That period, nighttime by the clock, is the best for photography, but it's the worst for climbing, since warmth creates snowmelt that drips down the wall, drenching whatever's beneath.

Further stressing my body clock, everyone wants time in front of the camera, and suspicions are growing about who is getting the most. Last night I spent eight hours belaying Jared with one hand and photographing him with the other. Then, when shadows crossed the face and Mark came up to lead the next pitch, I rappelled a thousand feet (300 m) back down to the ledge to sleep. No sooner did I doze off, however, than Alex woke me via radio; he was "jugging" up to lead after Mark. "Gordon, it's *spectacular* up here," he crooned. "You've *got* to come back up!" Even though clouds swirled everywhere and the light was gloomy and grey, I grumpily start spidering back up all the ropes I've just come down, as well as the 200 feet (60 m) that Mark led.

I should have delayed. Photography is always difficult from belay stances. Unless I can get off to the side, all I get are "butt shots." At least today Alex promises to set up a photography line for me and to reclimb some of the more dramatic moves. Still, he can only do so after he has inched up one of the wall's toughest sections. Greg, on belay, is cold, bored, and even more out of sorts than I am. We hang awkwardly squashed together for what seems an eternity.

For me, it's worth the wait. Once Alex runs out the rope and establishes anchors at a site that will soon become our hanging camp, he drops another line for me, pulls out his upper protection, and lowers himself back down to the most dramatic part of his pitch: a series of moves where he can progress only by placing "bat hooks" on tiny flakes. It looks horrifying through the camera and is obviously just as scary for Alex the second time around. I scoot up and down my rope to find the very best angles, and at times I even jump far out from the cliff so that I can look in and down—carefully gauging my leaps so I don't crash into Alex.

Meanwhile, the clouds have parted and it is close to 3 P.M. The sun is about to appear and I am salivating for better light. But waiting isn't easy. By now, Greg's patience is justifiably thin. Not only has he endured a long, uncomfortable belay, he has also spent several additional hours handling the rope as Alex, who could be considered a rival, dances in front of the camera.

1. As I hung from a rope that Alex Lowe had fixed earlier, he repeatedly climbed one of the more difficult portions of the upper headwall. In the first picture, he is reaching upward to feel what type of tool might hold his weight.

2. Alex places a “bat hook” over a small flake.

3. After moving up into sling ladders attached to the first hook, Alex places a second one at the next feasible location.

4. Alex steps over into a second set of sling ladders up which he will climb as far as he can maintain his balance before looking for another location to place a tool.

5. After waiting for two hours, dramatically different lighting emerged. I turned my wide-angle lens horizontal to include a background no longer hidden by fog.
6. To get a different perspective, I tried jumping out from the wall. Unfortunately, from this angle my own shadow crept into the frame.
7. In order to eliminate my shadow, I had to jump toward Alex, which made me worry that I would crash into him. Nevertheless, both of us were inspired by the light's beautiful texture, and he was willing to take the risk.

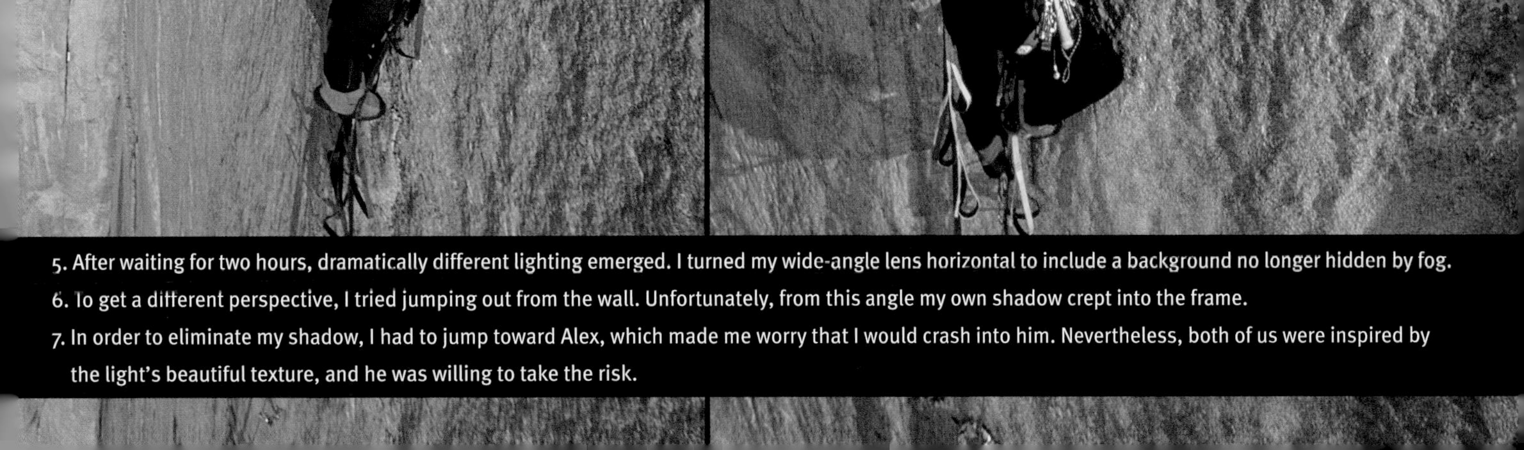

LEFT: Mark Synnott grimaces as he uses a complex pulley system to drag haul bags to our hanging camp. Jared Ogden, below, is acting as a counterweight.

TENUOUS TENTING

June 20, 1998 (Day 36)

Yesterday we hauled about half a ton of food, equipment, and water 1,200 feet (365 m) up to a huge overhang that will protect us from falling rocks and ice. We unfolded our portaledges and established a hanging bivouac that seems so far up the cliff that only birds could fly there.

An uninitiated person might think that we should be scared to camp here, but the tents are astonishingly snug and safe. Everything is redundantly rigged, and we never, ever, untie from our harnesses. It's a lot less frightening to sit inside (which seems just like any other tent) than to be outside, where I can see just how far above the ground we are. Nevertheless, vigilance is vital. If one of our hanging stoves flares up, it could torch our nylon walls in seconds, and there's always the worry of spilling a pot full of boiling water. What I hate most, however, is fetching something from our 4-foot-deep (1.3 m) haul bags. Whatever I need is always at the bottom, which means leaning far out from the tent, staring 2,400 feet (730 m) straight to the ground, and starting to burrow.

SPARRING FOR SPONSORSHIP

June 23, 1998 (Day 39)

Except for the first spectacular pitch above our hanging camp—the kind of clean, blank, overhanging granite that big wall climbers dream to visit—the last few days have become a blur. Bad weather has come and gone, we're running low on food and water, and one team or another is always on the go. We are beset with summit fever, and it is hard for me to ask anyone to re-climb anything. I worry that I still don't have any dramatic images of Mark, and I overhear grumbling from the portaledge he shares with Greg.

ABOVE: John Catto lights a hanging stove inside a portaledge.

OPPOSITE: The expedition's hanging camp, about 1,200 feet (365 m) above the big ledge below. An overhang protects the portaledges from falling rock and ice.

A5

OPPOSITE: Greg Child balances in slings on a very blank, tricky section of the upper headwall. This is the pitch that everyone wanted to lead.

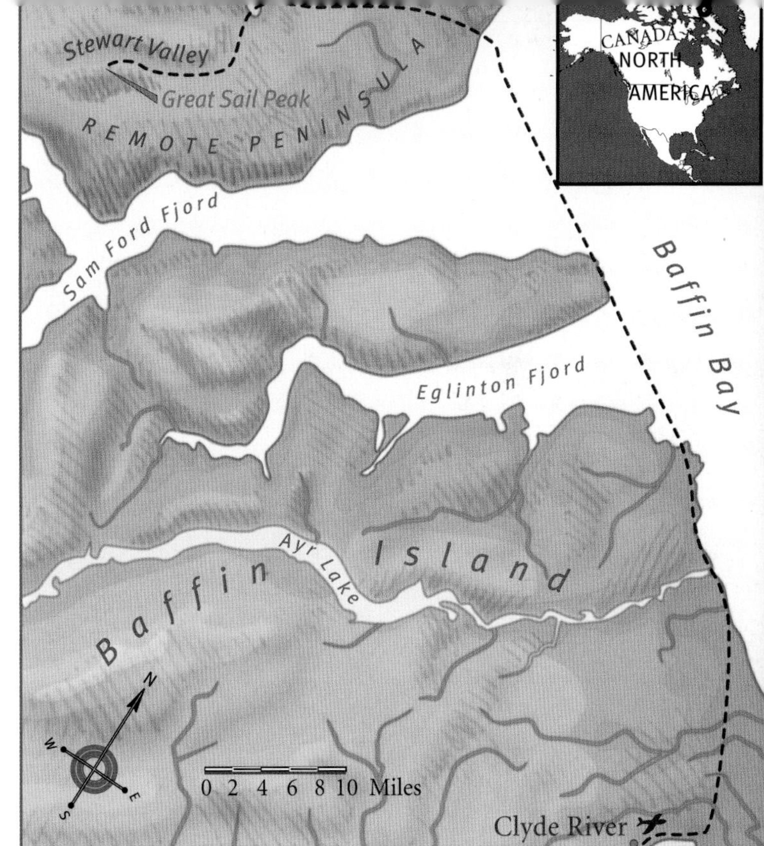

This isn't a laughing matter. Besides product testing, The North Face sponsors these climbers to get their faces and the company logo into print. What the others don't realize is that Alex is over-compensating for Queen Maud Land, where he ignored that reality and euphorically charged so far ahead of me that he almost didn't get a single climbing picture of himself into a twenty-four-page story. He isn't going to let *that* happen again, and since no one else is offering me even a fraction of the photographic assistance he is now providing, I'm trying not to feel guilty.

Further complicating things is that, as I found on the Queen Maud Land expedition, it is difficult to work in the same space and time as a videographer, whose lenses are at least as attractive to the climbers as my own. Ironically, neither John nor I is supposed to be included in the other's story, so it is a disaster when my flash—or the sound of my motor drive—ruins his video, or if my super-wide-angle lens captures any of his body or camera. Thankfully, we cooperate, laugh about these headaches, and enjoy each other's company in the portaledge we share.

A WELL-DESERVED NAP

June 25, 1998 (Day 41)

Alex and I are alone in camp, reading our books and listening to periodic radio reports from far above. We're hoping to reach the summit today; Jared is leading. Alex furrows his brow as Mark describes a giant loose block impeding progress. But somehow Jared wiggles around it and sees straight sailing to a ledge that seems to be less than 200 feet (60 m) from the top. Alex throws on his climbing clothes, laces his shoes, and swings skyward onto the fixed ropes. I've never seen anybody jumar so fast.

Mark is already leading the last, blocky pitch by the time I reach the ledge. John is filming and everyone is elated. Mark wants very badly to be the first on top, but his rope wraps around so many edges that just 30 feet (10 m) from the summit rim so much friction has built up that he can pull it no farther. Traditionally, this means a new pitch, and it is Alex's turn to lead. Mark feels short-changed and argues, but Alex takes the pitch. Ten minutes later he's on the summit plateau and I scamper upward to photograph the others arriving. To my chagrin, the last-minute tiff mushroomed into animosity. The others think that Alex is trying to hog all the glory. As they arrive at the top, each can only grudgingly shake his hand.

Nevertheless, there's nothing like a hard-earned summit to assuage hard feelings. By the time we've strolled the last, low-angle stretch to a boulder marking our mountain's highest point, it's high fives all around. And then, as if drugged by the warm spring sun, all of us fall asleep.

Alex Lowe departs from our hanging camp en route to the final summit push.

OPPOSITE: The expedition team atop Great Sail Peak. I shot the picture from an adjacent arête.

A youngster plays by his family's corral in the Darhad Valley.

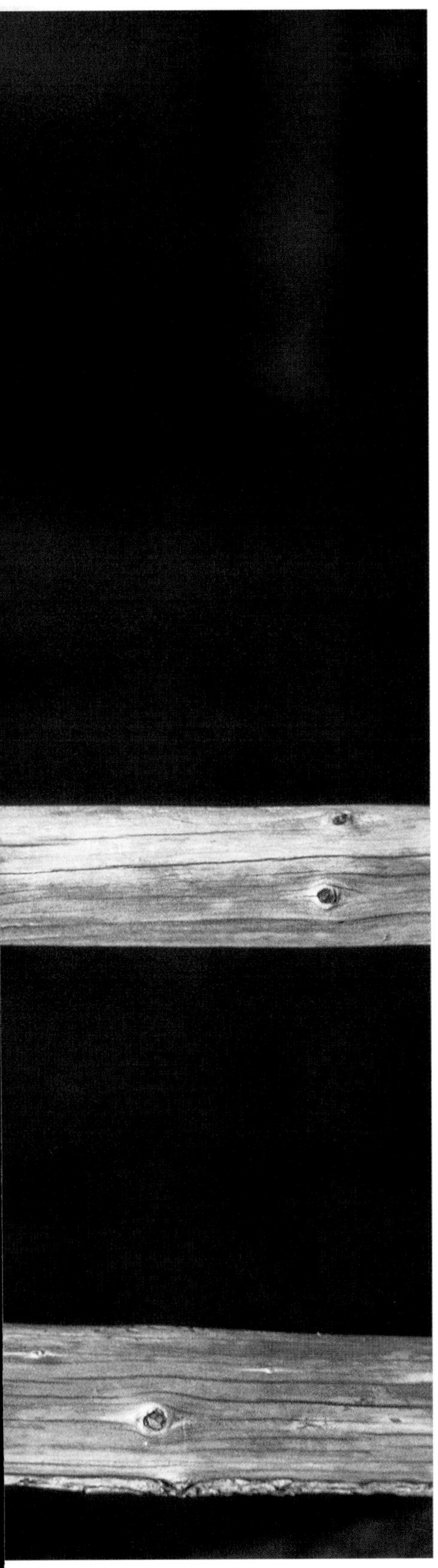

CHAPTER NINE

IN THE FOOTSTEPS OF GENGHIS KHAN

A Migration over Ancient Trails, Darhad Valley, Mongolia, 2002

- ***Location:*** The Darhad Valley, northern Mongolia; 51° N, 99° E; approximately 400 miles (670 km) west-northwest of Ulaanbaator
- ***Team:*** An entire culture. Accompanying me were Dr. Cliff Montagne, a professor of soil science at Montana State University in Bozeman; Temuulen "Teki" Tsagaan, a Mongolian-born graduate student under Cliff's mentorship; Mishig Jigjidsuren, the first popularly elected regional governor (now retired) of the postsocialist era; Glenn Hodges, a *National Geographic* staff writer; Chinbat, a facilitator from our outfitter, Boojum Expeditions; Achit, an interpreter for Glenn; and Maagi, our expedition cook.*
- ***Dates:*** September 13 to November 3, 2002, round-trip from Ulaanbaator
- ***Conditions:*** A quickly cooling mix, beginning with warm and balmy sun, changing to frigid winter, with blizzard winds exceeding 70 mph (100 kph) and temperatures dipping to −30°F (−35°C)

FROM TIMES BEFORE WRITTEN HISTORY, nomadic herders of the Darhad Valley in northern Mongolia have constantly moved their flocks of sheep, goats, camels, cattle, yaks, oxen, and horses from one grazing area to another. Most are short moves, perhaps taking even less than a day, and their *gers,* sturdy, round, felt-lined houses, are designed for mobility. (Americans call these "yurts," but that is actually a Russian word despised by Mongolians.) When freezing winter winds begin to pile up snowy drifts, however, conditions in the Darhad become so fierce that almost everyone migrates over the rugged, 10,000-foot (3,000 m) Horidal Saridag Mountains to the heavily forested slopes above Lake Hovsgol, where temperatures are moderated by thermal inversions above this massive feeder to Russia's nearby Lake Baikal.

* Customarily, everyone in Mongolia is called by a singular given name; their family one is seldom used.

OPPOSITE: A young herder plays hide and seek around her family's ger beside Dood Nuur, a lake. The motorcycle is a sign of both wealth and changing times that may threaten the region's nomadic lifestyle.

(Both lakes are still among the largest, purest bodies of water on earth.) Come spring, when the Darhad begins to turn green, these nomads migrate back. In both fall and spring, the travelers are often beset by blizzard-force winds and heavy snow. Some years, many people die.

Mass migrations are rapidly disappearing elsewhere, but the Darhad Mongols persevere and are proud of their heritage, which includes a dialect of their own. Few outside of the immediate region, however, had even heard of this twice-a-year event. In summer 2001, Dr. Cliff Montagne, his wife Joan, and his Mongolian-born graduate student, Teki Tsagaan, were confronted by the region's former governor, Mishig, who showed them children's sketches of the cavalcade and asked why no one had ever photographed it.

Cliff passed the question to me, and I forwarded it to Kent Kobersteen, the director of photography at *National Geographic.* Although this was not the type of expedition I was best-known for photographing, it promised similar hardships, and in many ways was more appealing than rock climbs, ski traverses, and other adventures that could be perceived as frivolous by comparison. In these Mongolian mountains, more than one thousand people and one hundred thousand animals risk their lives twice a year—not for fun, but because it is the only way for them to survive. Ultimately, the senior editors agreed that I might perform well on the project and sent me to the region for almost

A veterinarian weighs an animal as part of a fall checkup on the herd.

two months, accompanied by Cliff, Teki, Mishig, three Mongolians to work as support staff, and Glenn Hodges, a young staff writer for the magazine.

One of Mishig's goals was to bring more attention to the Darhad Valley—a setting that closely resembles my home state of Montana, one hundred years ago. As a business partner in Boojum Expeditions, which he co-owns with my friends Kent Madin and Linda Svendsen from Bozeman, he had begun to profit from ecotourists, who came to ride horses and catch huge fish, but the region still remained obscure, with no hotels, nonexistent scheduled transportation, and scarely a mention in earlier editions of Lonely Planet's *Mongolia.* Mishig had seen too many youngsters flee this beautiful valley to chase often unfulfilled dreams in the city of Ulaanbaator. Why not use the natural resources surrounding him to inspire local pride, attract more tourists, and make a better life for a culture that predates the American Wild West by millennia?

FOLLOWING SPREAD: **The Horidal Saridag Mountains are now part of Lake Hovsgol National Park. Hovsgol remains one of deepest, clearest lakes on earth and is often called "BabyBaikal" after the larger Russian lake into which it drains.**

LEFT: Battogtokh and her husband, Dorjgoo, enjoy salty tea during a break from making felt. Both were veterinarians who became herders after the collapse of Soviet-sponsored collectivization.

BELOW: A traditional Mongolian saddle is propped against a felt-lined ger. In the distance is a "scare wolf," constructed to protect the family's sheep.

RIGHT: Young jockeys gallop bareback on their families' fastest horses during a naadam race.

STAMPEDING THE STEPPES

September 18, 2002 (Day 6)

Today Cliff sponsored a *naadam,* a festival that drew nearly a thousand people to Renchinlhumbe, the capital, and one of only two towns in the Darhad region. He wanted to express his thanks to the people who helped with his and Teki's research, and to introduce me to them. He believed they might otherwise shun someone who was staring at them through a camera's glass eye. After formal speeches via bullhorn, for which both Cliff and I memorized lines in Mongolian, the events began: wrestling, archery, chess, and horse racing.

Although my riding experience is limited, my favorite event at the naadam is the horse racing. Equestrian mastery was the means by which Genghis Khan and his hordes ran rough-shod over most of the known world in the thirteenth century. Winning a race is a source of great family pride, and confers valuable breeding rights to champion horses. I rent a steed, which knows I am a greenhorn, and ride about 10 miles (15 km) to the starting line, mixing in with the bareback, barefoot contestants, most of whom are under age ten.

Once the race begins, I can scarcely believe how quickly the horses gallop past me, much less the seemingly instinctive abilities of their prepubescent jockeys, who are steering with one hand and whipping with the other. I set up for a picture and briefly think they will pummel me into the ground. The next moment they are gone. There is much pushing and shoving, and children fly off their mounts, which run on to town without them. A Toyota picks up the thrown riders.

LEFT: Nyamdalai, a wrestler in traditional costume.

BELOW: Judges keep a close watch as one wrestler trounces another.

Wrestling is the next most popular attraction, and another national sport. The rules are simple. In a ritual with shamanistic overtones, each contestant flaps his arms like bird wings, eyeballs the other, and then tries to knock his opponent off his feet. You lose if any other body part touches the ground, but in some cases an unlucky victim will get resoundingly flipped and pounded onto his back, an outcome that usually triggers cheers and raucous laughter from the crowd. Each winner then challenges the others until a field of about eighty is narrowed to a single champion and runner-up. Although some men wrestle in street clothes, most serious contenders wear tight, brightly colored shorts to prove they have no cleavage. No one wants to repeat a past *naadam,* when a woman in disguise won the event and humiliated all the men.

The winning wrestler at the Renchinlhumbe naadam festival tosses fermented mare's milk to celebrate.

I don't spend much film photographing chess, which is about as visually exciting as watching paint dry. Archery, on the other hand, is far more exhilarating, especially when the participants drink too much fermented mare's milk. Most contestants have a dead-eye, as evidenced by how closely the judges stand around a small circle where arrows are supposed to land. Afterward, however, anyone can take a shot—many of them straight up.

OPPOSITE: Umgan, a shaman, beats his drum, dances, and chants to put himself into the trance that enables him to divine the future of migrating families, treat illnesses, or otherwise minister to his community's spiritual needs.

ENTRANCED

September 22, 2002 (Day 10)

Our task now is to document life as it has always been in the Darhad Valley. Today we take a log raft across a small river to ask Umgan, a shaman, to bless us. His wife serves salt-laden tea while she scurries to warm, and thereby dry, his ageless skin drum so that it will emit exactly the correct pitch.

With much ceremony, he dons an elaborate costume that he keeps hidden in a trunk. He's not worried about theft, but is simply acting out of habits left over from the days when Josef Stalin encouraged his despotic Mongolian puppet to shoot shamans and Buddhist monks on sight. When at last the shaman is properly adorned in colorful robes, a mask, and false hair that covers his eyes, he tosses pinches of vodka in the four primary directions and picks up a drumstick made from wood and a rabbit's foot. After one loud boom, he puts his head inside the drum and softly begins tapping it.

"Are there any devils here?" he demands, seemingly entranced from mare's milk, burning incense, and what might be heavenly magic. After another boom! he launches into a language that is gibberish to all but his wife and his daughter, to whom his powers will pass. I am terrified that the electronic flashes I have devised to capture his movements will destroy the moment.

Despite my intrusion, he relays that the spirits have told him our journey will be successful, but difficult. Nevertheless, he deeply scares Maagi, our cook, when he says that she will soon suffer a personal tragedy. Her daughter has a baby on the way, and Maagi wonders if she should leave us and return to her home in Möron.

Tibetan Buddhism, once a widespread religion in Mongolia, was nearly exterminated under Communism. Today there is only one elderly monk in Renchinlhumbe.

THE RUNAWAY

September 29, 2002 (Day 17)

Today Teki, Cliff, and I explore the boarding school at Renchinlhumbe. One positive aspect of Soviet "assistance" to Mongolia was an infusion of money to build schools everywhere, which they claimed raised the country's literacy rate to an astonishing 97 percent. Even today it remains well above 90 percent, a source of great national pride. Even children of nomadic families attend the school, and many are separated from their parents for five or six months a year. Often families will trade off which children travel to help with the herds and which stay in school.

Younger schoolchildren share dorm rooms with their brothers, sisters, and cousins. Older students are separated by gender. Upon touring some of the halls, however, I can see that this place could be lonely. Uuganjii, a man who now works for Mishig, became so alarmed when his parents migrated toward Lake Hovsgol that he sneaked out of the dorm and ran 18 miles (25 km) to try to catch them, eventually collapsing in the snow from exhaustion. If he had not been found early the next morning by a hunter, he certainly would have perished. Despite losing both legs and most of his fingers to frostbite, he later made his own wooden legs, learned to handle tools with what was left of his hands, and went on to become the town's most reliable carpenter.

LEFT, ABOVE: Lonely youngsters at the boarding school in Renchinlhumbe.

LEFT: When Uuganjii was twelve years old, his family left him in school while they migrated. He pursued them on foot through the snow, nearly perished from hypothermia, and lost most of his fingers and both legs to frostbite.

The preschool building in Renchinlhumbe, with the Horidal Saridag Mountains in the background.

ABOVE: Chuluunkhuu, a young herder, waits in his family's ger as his sister Delgersaikahn prepares a flat bread she will roll into noodles and boil with sheep fat into a stew. Few crops are grown locally and vegetables are seldom available.

BELOW: Batnasan leads her flock through the forest en route to Horidal Pass.

SETTING FORTH

October 8, 2002 (Day 26)

We wake long before dawn to accompany a tough, middle-aged woman named Batnasan, her family, and her flocks across Horidal Pass, the southernmost of three migrations routes. This is their third day on what she suspects will be a week-long journey. Batnasan is a proud and worldly woman, hardened by the recent death of her husband. She is seriously short-handed without her husband's strength and eagle-eye with a gun (wolves are a legitimate fear), so she is migrating earlier than most of her neighbors in order to ensure grazing for her sizeable herds, as well as to avoid getting trapped in a storm. Most nomads wait until the ground freezes more solidly, to ensure better footing for their animals across the permafrost. I am astonished that the family can disassemble their ger, pack their yaks and oxen, and get underway in less than two hours. It is barely dawn as they switch-back up a trail between towering limestone mountains.

By Mongolian standards, Batnasan is a wealthy woman who owns hundreds of animals. They push, butt, and shove each other in front of my camera, bellowing cries of "moo," "baa," "neigh," and the like. To my vast relief, the weather is good and, at the absolute most scenic point dawn light paints the mountains pink. With the aid of electronic flashes, special filters, and my subjects' good humor, I capture the scene.

BELOW: The ancient migration route from Darhad Valley to Horidal Pass.

OPPOSITE: A woman lights her stove below Utreg Pass as her family sets up camp and tends to the animals outside.

A BABY IN A BOX

October 14, 2002 (Day 32)

"Gordon! You've got to see this!" cries Teki. I rush out of our rented ger and race to her side, where she is surrounded by the bustle of a large family packing up for their fourth day on the move. There, swaddled in sheepskin, is two-year-old Enkhee, snuggled into a crib-sized box and lovingly watched by his older brother Dalai, age five, and sister Jagai, four. The scene is adorable, barely lit by a deep red sunrise. Cliff helps to string out flashes and fiddle with filters, and I try to capture what seems an impossible image. When I have finished, Enkhee's father and uncle scoop up his box and lash it to the back of a yak they say is especially gentle. For most of the day he will stay snuggled in the box, unattended in a large bovine herd as his relatives thrash back and forth through the woods chasing down wayward beasts. Dalai and Jagai, whose feet can barely reach their stirrups, will ride their own horses all day.

By this point snow covers the ground and temperatures seldom rise above 10°F (–12°C). Mishig has driven us about 40 miles (70 km) north of Horidal Pass to Utreg Pass, the northernmost migration route. Several families a day are now moving across each of the three passes, their timing scheduled in some previously agreed-upon manner to avoid congestion either on the trails or at vital grazing areas.

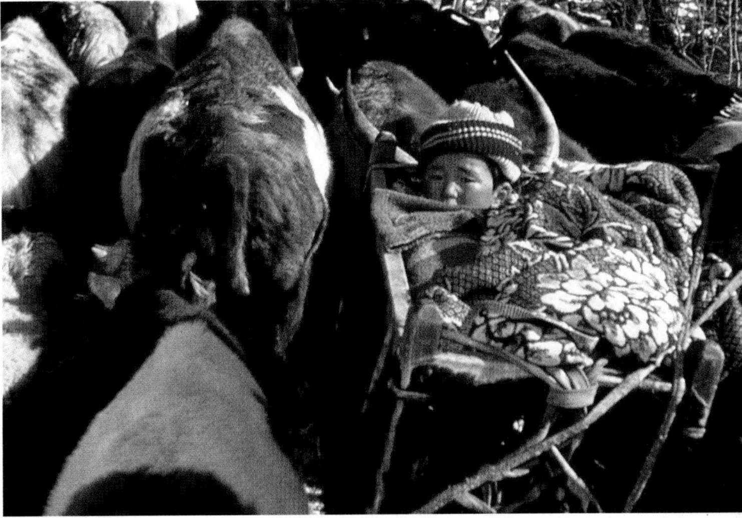

RIGHT, TOP TO BOTTOM: While their family packs for the day's journey, Dalai and Jagai watch over two-year-old Enkhee, who will ride in a box on the back of a yak.

Four generations of migrating herders (from left): eighty-eight-year-old Dashingaa, her granddaughter Javsan, great-granddaughter Otgonjii, and daughter Darisuren, age seventy.

A two-year-old child rides up 8,000-foot (2,450 m) Utreg Pass on the back of an unattended yak as his parents chase down stray animals. The youngster arrived safely, but some small children smother or are crushed when animals stampede.

Seventy-year-old Darisuren sets off with her small flock for the trek across Utreg Pass. Because her family is poor, she does not own a horse and has to walk the entire 60-mile (100 km) distance.

As nightfall approaches, thirteen-year-old Boldbaatar unloads an ox at Tsol Meadows. After a rudimentary meal and a few hours sleep, his family will disassemble their ger and hit the trail again, long before dawn.

Cliff, Teki, and I ride with Enkhee's family most of the way to the following camp. The weather is constantly changing, with moments of sun, snow, cold, and fleeting warmth. Nevertheless, the atmosphere is festive, and I enjoy watching as older teenage boys poke each other's horses in the butt to see if they can make them buck. I pray they don't do the same to me; I know they would howl if I hit the ground. There are moments of frustration, such as when a fully laden ox walks between two trees spaced narrower than its load, knocking everything off. Never do I hear an angry word.

My biggest challenge is trying to photograph Enkhee in his box. My horse doesn't like walking among the yaks and oxen, where long, sharp horns poke in every direction. I try to steer with one hand while using the other to adjust my flash and other settings and try to compose a perfect frame, which means urging my constantly-bouncing horse to move as little as a foot or more in one direction or another. After shooting several rolls, we take a break. As I dismount, my steed immediately expresses her frustration by trying to kick Cliff, whom I suspect she mistakes for me.

SAFE PASSAGE

October 23, 2002 (Day 41)

Today we finally make it over Utreg Pass. More snow has fallen, and the last families are scurrying upward, where Mishig, Cliff, Teki, and I have focused our efforts. We awake to a modest blizzard and saddle up to follow about a thousand animals on a route that will take us within just a few miles of the Russian border.

I have become a significantly better rider, which

OPPOSITE: A wealthy family's sheep and goats scramble across 8,000-foot (2,450 m) Utreg Pass.

proves vital as we gallop through brush, snowy rocks, and the occasional ice-choked stream to get ahead of the herds. It is easy to see why people—including some of the babies in boxes—often die every year. The mercury has dropped far below 0°F (–20°C), and at any moment it seems as if the clouds could descend and trap everyone in a whiteout, where individual animals and family members could become separated and subsequently freeze to death.

To everyone's relief, the storm dissipates rather than intensifies, and I get beautiful pictures of animals wallowing through knee-deep snow (belly-deep on the sheep). Atop the pass the route flattens onto a long, high plateau and the herds that have gone ahead have created a moderate trail. As before, the atmosphere is festive, with much joking and horseplay and no one seems to get too cold. After many hours we descend again to lower elevations, regain the forests, and spend the night with two families that have now become our good friends. Our adventures are nearly at an end. Mishig does not want us to travel any farther; it is not uncommon for riders to suffer broken bones when their horses slip on hidden ice and fall on them. On our return trip, we would be alone much of the way and any mishap could prove fatal.

THE BIG BAD WOLF

October 29, 2002 (Day 47)

As a final excursion, Mishig wanted us to meet some of his relatives who live in far western Darhad. Instead of migrating east to Lake Hovsgol, this clan moves west into mountains very close to Russia.

Although these people welcome us, some are angry. Two nights before, an armed Tuvan posse sneaked over the border, rounded up twenty-five of their best horses, and beat a hasty retreat. If our new friends had awoken, there doubtless would have been gunfire.

Further heightening emotions, the next night a pack of wolves had come right into their camp and slaughtered at least a dozen sheep and goats—a tremendous financial blow. Everyone agreed that it was time for a hunt. To my astonishment, they invited Mishig, Teki, and me to join them. This great honor is seldom bestowed on either a foreigner or a woman.

OPPOSITE: A large herd ascends through deep snow into the wild and frigid Horidol Saridag Mountains.

Armed with old Russian carbines, the hunters galloped out of camp at midmorning in search of the freshest canine tracks, easy to find in new-fallen snow. Despite their ire, the mood was giddy. Everyone pushed their animals to gallop as quickly as possible, and I found myself in the center of the herd. Whenever my horse slowed even slightly, someone would whip it on the butt. I dreaded falling off and getting trampled. The embarrassment alone would be bad enough.

After about half an hour we veered up a steep slope and the chief tracker, who was also master of the hunt, spotted multiple tracks. Wolves had obviously passed this way recently and excitement skyrocketed. Except, perhaps, for breeding a champion horse or winning a wrestling match, there is no greater sign of manhood than killing a wolf.

We break into two groups. One, which includes the younger boys and less-experienced men, sneak east and hide as quietly as possible. The rest of us fan out a mile (2 km) or so west. When everyone is in place, the eastern group starts walking toward us, banging pans and shouting to drive any animals to the guns. Mishig, Teki, and I are each stationed with a hunter and ordered not to move a muscle. Ultimately we see a deer, but no wolves, a fact that did not disappoint me. The hunting party, however, did likely give the wolf pack a good scare, which was as much the point as anything.

Teki and I leave the hunting party early and begin a gradual descent back into the Darhad, in order to meet our transport out of Renchinlhumbe. The light is magnificent, but I feel as if my job is done. I put away my camera and simply enjoy the ride. Far below us men and women on horses are rounding up yaks, sheep, goats, and other animals. I can see no evidence of anything from the twenty-first century. The Horidal Saridag Mountains glisten blue and white in the distance, log corrals surround golden piles of hay, and nearly virgin forests cover the intermediate hills. If not for my wristwatch and cameras, I could have been riding into a Montana cow camp a century ago. I am mesmerized, and as we spur our mounts into the last gallop of our journey, I realize that this has been the most rewarding expedition of my life.

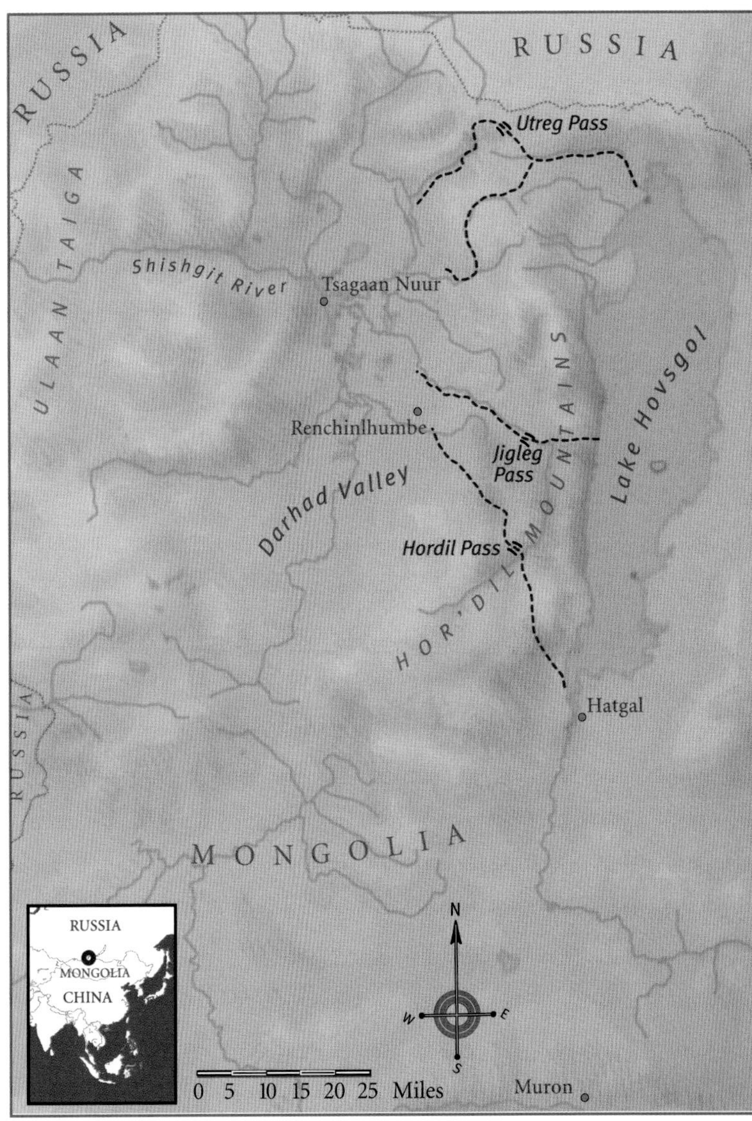

1

2

3

4

5

Captions for pages 18–19.

1. A nomadic woman from the Larkya region of Nepal.
2. Jarkot village and Yak Face Mountain, north of Annapurna in Nepal.
3. Thousands of Hindus converge on Patan Durbar Square in the Kathmandu Valley to pray during Krishna's birthday.
4. An eighty-year-old farmer in the Kali Gandaki Gorge, below Annapurna.
5. One-year-old Baterdenye rides on an ox, often unattended, during his family's long migration from Mongolia's Darhad Valley over the Horidal Saridag Mountains to Lake Hovsgol.
6. A Uygur youngster eats lunch in a tiny café in Muq, a small bazaar town near Kashgar.
7. Uygur school girls in Kashgar, Xinjiang, China.
8. Tibetan masked dancers in Kathmandu.
9. Ski mountaineers Jay Jensen and Allan Pietrasanta pack up during an expedition to ski across the Great Himalaya Range. A week later, I broke my back in an avalanche and had to help them rescue me by skiing under my own power 20 miles (33 km) to the nearest town.
10. The Cordillera Sarmiento Expedition team hides from a blizzard with hurricane-force winds inside a soggy snow cave.
11. Long-time climbing partners Alex Lowe and Conrad Anker share a tent in the Ellsworth Mountains, Antarctica.
12. The Queen Maud Land Expedition team celebrates their departure from Cape Town after long delays.
13. Wolves were howling nearby as I photographed this aurora borealis over my tent on frozen Great Slave Lake in Canada's Northwest Territories.

Captions for pages 22–23.

1. Sanu Thapa, a traditional Nepali singer in Kathmandu.
2. A village elder from Kanji village in the Zanskar Mountains of Ladakh.
3. Khokrii, a young Mongolian nomad who is training to be a shaman under the tutelage of her father, Umgan.
4. A nomadic Mongolian family's children ride in a box atop a yak.
5. Maximilliano Siccha, a homesteader in the upper Amazonian drainages of Peru.
6. Jay Jensen in 100 mph (165 kph) winds at about 23,000 feet (7,000 m) on Baruntse Peak, Nepal.
7. A Hindu yogi on a five-day pilgrimage to Amarnath Cave in the Great Himalaya Range, Kashmir.
8. A young Tibetan in the Tsangpo River Gorge holds a gold amulet with a forbidden picture of the Dalai Lama.
9. Sherpa elder Konchok Chombi sits by a window in Namche Bazaar. Years ago, he took a treasured "yeti" scalp abroad to England for study.
10. A Peruvian fruit vendor spins wool as she waits for customers near Chachapoyas, in the Amazonas district.
11. A Tibetan Buddhist dancer relaxes during a ceremony blessing international traders who live in the Manang Valley north of Annapurna, Nepal.
12. Mongolian herder Chorlee shows off a homemade "scare wolf" he built to frighten predators that eat his sheep and other animals in the Darhad Valley.
13. A Hindu *jhankri* (witch doctor) hikes in his costume near Takshindo Monastery, in the Solu region of Nepal.
14. Danish dog musher Ulrik Vedel endures –45°F (–42°C) breezes beside the Arctic Ocean at Cape Arkticheskiy on Severnaya Zemlya archipelago, Russia.
15. Nomadic Gujar herdsman in the Great Himalaya Range near Pahalgam, Kashmir.
16. Young Tibetan Buddhist monks pray in a new *gompa* (temple) near Bodh'nath Stupa in the Kathmandu Valley.

Captions for pages 218–219.

1. Seventy-six-year-old Sharkhuukhed shares a quiet moment with her grandson Uuganzaya, age three.
2. Seventy-five-year-old Gonchigsuren relaxes in his ger with his cat and his pipe.
3. Costumed riders head out to race at a naadam festival in Renchinlhumbe, the largest town in Darhad Valley.
4. Young herders struggle to put a wooden peg that will act as a bridle through the nostril of one of their camels. Seconds later—to everyone's delight—the animal spat a mouthful of horrible green slime all over me and my camera.
5. A wealthy father and son watch Russian television programs received via a satellite dish they pack on a camel. By glamorizing city life, television may be the single greatest threat to the survival of the nomads' traditional ways.

ACKNOWLEDGMENTS

EXPEDITION PHOTOGRAPHY is always a team effort, and in the span of my career I have depended on ever-changing human chains of players—from famous leaders to anonymous, barefoot porters. Above and beyond the most obvious people that I have mentioned in these pages—all of whom deserve enormous gratitude—there are so many others who have contributed to the pictures in this book that it would be impossible to list them: my teachers, sponsors, clients, friends, mentors, editors, lab techs, shopkeepers, designers, and others almost ad infinitum.

On the other hand, this book, as a specific printed entity, is a direct consequence of a small but tightly coordinated team that brought it to life, and I would like to acknowledge a few key players. First and foremost, I want to thank my editor, John Barstow, with whom I have worked for years as a photographer and who finally generated the underlying premise of *To the Ends of the Earth.* Altogether, he spent more than two years convincing me (and, more importantly, the editorial board at W. W. Norton) that I should write down the photographer's point of view on the stories behind my pictures. Without his hands-on guidance, judicious red pencil, and enormous enthusiasm, this book might never have sparked into reality.

Similarly, I want to thank my agent, Peter Matson, who helped to steer me through various other misguided ideas and finally worked closely with John to focus my attention on this project instead.

To my brief dismay, John made the painful decision to leave Norton (which feels more like a family than a business) to work for another publisher closer to his beloved home in Vermont; but he did stick with my book as a guardian angel and cleverly guided further responsibilities for the edited manuscript and stack of pictures to Morgen Van Vorst, who added a passion all her own. Without her help, I could never have navigated—much less even guessed—all of the myriad details a finished book involves!

My readers should also be grateful to copy editor Kristin Sperber, who not only straightened out my sometimes-convoluted sentences but also worked to learn enough about wilderness activities and history that she caught an astonishing variety of arcane factual errors. I am especially indebted, too, to book designer Beth Tondreau at BTDNYC, whose magnificent composition and attention to detail led to a wonderful marriage of words and images. The product of her work is greater than the sum of its parts!

There are many, many other people at W. W. Norton who deserve my thanks as well, and I heartily extend it.

Furthermore, I owe profound gratitude to my other "family" at the National Geographic Society, a remarkable team that has helped to make some of my wildest dreams come true. I promised not to get carried away naming names, and nowhere is that more difficult to keep than here. So many people at the society have done so much for me that it is almost impossible not to mention some, such as Bert, Peter, Rebecca, Kent, Susan, John, Bill, Priit, Bruce, Rob, Chris, Maura, Greg, Jim, and a further list that could go on for pages.

Closer to home, I wouldn't have lasted long in my own business (AlpenImage, Ltd.) without someone to run it during my constant absences. In addition to my wife and business partner, Meredith, I will also always be indebted to my longtime assistant Linda Hausler for years of creative service and never-ending solutions to ever-changing crises.

Finally, I'd have gotten nowhere without the devotion of my family, especially Meredith. So many times, when I felt battered and bruised, she got me back on my feet and back in the harness, even when it was sometimes fun for neither of us. I love her deeply and I owe her everything. It is to her and our sons, Benjamin and Nicholas, that I dedicate this book.

INDEX

Page numbers in *italics* refer to illustrations.